Commentary on Romans

Letters of Commentary to Fellow Believers on the Epistle to the Romans

Carl Manthey Zorn

Translated by Richard A. Riess
Edited by Linda (Riess) Young and Timothy Koch

Cover Design: Andrea L. Schultz
Copyright © 2018 Linda Riess Young

Scripture quotations are from the ESV® Bible (The Holy Bible, English Standard Version®), copyright 2001 by Crossway, a publishing ministry of Good News Publishers. Used by permission. All rights reserved.

All rights reserved. No part of this publication may be reproduced, stored in a retrieval system, or transmitted, in any form or by any means, electronic, mechanical, photocopying, recording, or otherwise, without the prior written permission of Linda Riess Young.

Zorn, Carl Manthey, 1846–1928.
    Letters of Commentary to Fellow Believers on the Epistle to the Romans / by Carl Manthey Zorn; translated by Richard A Riess.
    Translation of *Der Brief an die Römer in Briefen an Glaubensbrüder*, which was published in Zwickau by J. Hermann [1923].

1. Bible. N.T. Romans—Commentaries

Manufactured in the United States of America

ISBN-13: 978-1725981638

For I am not ashamed of the gospel, for it is the power of God for salvation to everyone who believes.

~Romans 1:16a~

The doubtful feeling, Lord, I beg of you;
let it be foreign to my soul.
It is like a boat on the water away from shore
that the wind tosses to and fro.
Give me a strong sense and cheerful courage
that nothing will take me away from You.
A heart that will always believe in You
and endure until the end.

~Translation of a German prayer taped to the inside cover of Richard Riess's copy of the presently translated volume~

CONTENTS

Foreword i
Editors' Preface iii
Biography v

Zorn's Commentary on Romans

Introduction (Romans 1:1–2) 1
Letter I (Romans 1:3–7) 3
Letter II (Romans 1:8–17) 6
Letter III (Romans 1:18–32) 10
Letter IV (Romans 2:1–5) 14
Letter V (Romans 2:6–16) 17
Letter VI (Romans 2:17–29) 21
Letter VII (Romans 3:1–8) 25
Letter VIII (Romans 3:9–20) 29
Letter IX (Romans 3:21–26) 32
Letter X (Romans 3:27–31) 37
Letter XI (Romans 4) 41
Letter XII (Romans 5:1–11) 45
Letter XIII (Romans 5:12–21) 48
Letter XIV (Romans 6:1–14) 52
Letter XV (Romans 6:15–23) 56
Letter XVI (Romans 7:1–6) 60
Letter XVII (Romans 7:7–13) 65
Letter XVIII (Romans 7:14–25) 70
Letter XIX (Romans 8:1–17) 74
Letter XX (Romans 8:18–27) 79
Letter XXI (Romans 8:28–39) 85
Letter XXII (Romans 9:1–13) 90
Letter XXIII (Romans 9:14–18) 95
Letter XXIV (Romans 9:19–29) 100
Letter XXV (Romans 9:30–10:21) 106
Letter XXVI (Romans 11:1–10) 110
Letter XXVII (Romans 11:11–15) 114
Letter XXVIII (Romans 11:16–24) 118
Letter XXIX (Romans 11:25–32) 122
Letter XXX (Romans 11:33–36) 125

Letter XXXI (Romans 12) 128
Letter XXXII (Romans 13) 132
Letter XXXIII (Romans 14) 135
Letter XXXIV (Romans 15:1–13) 140
Letter XXXV (Romans 15:14–33) 143
Letter XXXVI (Romans 16) 147

Foreword

My father, Richard A. Riess, loved people. But, most of all, he loved his Lord and Savior, Jesus Christ. During his fifty-plus years of active ministry in the Lutheran Church—Missouri Synod, he served congregations large and small in Michigan, Wyoming, Oregon, and Washington. His joy was to serve as an ambassador for Christ wherever he went. He was always looking for a way to reach people with the Christian gospel.

The following translation of Carl Manthey Zorn's *Der Brief an die Römer in Briefen an Glaubensbrüder* is another way he hoped to spread the gospel. He first became acquainted with the commentary during his pastoral training at Concordia Seminary, St. Louis, possibly as a text book. He labored on the translation during his retirement years, writing meticulously in long-hand on both sides of legal-sized sheets, even during periods of hospitalization. He would send me envelopes of chapters he had finished so I could type them—no word processors were available at the time. When he finished the project, there were 214 chock-full, hand-written pages. He strongly believed that the material would be especially good for laymen's Bible study since Zorn's style is devotional and written in a conversational, easy-to-understand way.

I finally transcribed the entire book during my first year of retirement and looked for a way to keep my promise to make it available to other Christians. My friend, Dr. Gerhard Bode, Dean of Advanced Studies, Associate Professor of Historical Theology and Concordia Seminary Archivist, directed me to Rev. Timothy Koch. So, after more than a year of searching for an editor, I contacted Rev. Koch, who took a chance to work with a stranger and ordinary layman on a very large, detailed, and time-consuming project. He serves a dual-point parish in South Dakota so has a full pastoral schedule of his own. Without his special expertise, hard work, and patience this book might never have come to be.

I am indebted to him and to Dr. Bode for their help. I am also indebted to my husband Phillip, whom I'd like to thank for his continual encouragement. He is the eternal optimist and his loving encouragement, even when I hit brick walls and rejections, has kept me going.

My father would be the first to say that whatever we have accomplished was with the Lord's help and to His glory alone. I pray that God will use these pages to warn and to comfort through His Word as written in Romans.

Soli Deo gloria.

~Linda (Riess) Young

EDITOR'S PREFACE

I am a copy-editor. That alone is my role in the production of this present volume. As stated in the Foreword, this book was translated from German into English by Rev. Richard A. Riess. My own skills with German are very limited. Except for a single otherwise unintelligible passage in this book, I did not check the translation for accuracy or consistency. Frankly, I'm not qualified to do so. I blindly trusted the translation of the late Rev. Richard A. Riess.

In editing this book I tried to let the translation stand as is. German is a wordy language with a seemingly infinite number of subordinating clauses in any given sentence. Except for rare instances, I did not trim these down for the ease of reading, nor did I remove many redundancies.

Though I am a pastor in the Lutheran Church—Missouri Synod, I did not make any changes to the theology presented herein. I made no editorial changes for the sake of clarifying the law or the gospel. I tried to let Zorn's words stand as he wrote them. Any objections to the theology of this book will have to be taken up with Zorn himself after the day of the resurrection of all flesh.

Der Brief an die Römer in Briefen an Glaubensbrüder was published without a publication date. Thanks to the research of Lyle Buettner, former special collections librarian at Concordia Seminary, we can estimate the original publication to 1923.

The prayer that is presented before this book's table of contents was written in German. It was translated into English by Mrs. Hedi Swanhorst of Aberdeen, SD, and we thank her for doing so.

There were a four instances where Rev. Richard A. Riess did not translate the titles of the chapters. My thanks to Rev. David Juhl of Our Savior Lutheran Church in Momence, IL for utilizing his German skills to translate those for us.

Occasionally throughout this book you will find words in italics. These words were emphasized by the translator Rev. Richard A. Riess. There were no typographical emphases in the original publication.

Carl Manthey Zorn occasionally cites hymns. Some of them are still found in Lutheran hymnals today, some of them are not. Thanks to the website hymnary.org, I was able to discover that every single one of these hymns (except "Auf, Christenmensch auf auf zum Streit") was included in the *Kirchen-Gesangbuch für Evangelische-Lutherische Gemeinden*—a hymnal published by the Evangelical Lutheran Synod of Missouri, Ohio, and other States in St. Louis, Missouri in 1862. Thus, when the stanza number is provided in a footnote, the cited stanza number corresponds to the stanza number as it was found in that 1862 hymnal.

Soli Deo gloria.

~Rev. Timothy Koch

A Brief Biography of Carl Manthey Zorn

Carl Manthey Zorn was a Lutheran pastor who was born in Germany in 1846 and served as a missionary to India from 1871–1876. After a falling out with his fellow missionaries over their denial in the doctrine of the Trinity, Zorn returned to Germany to a cool reception in Erlangen. Having corresponded with C. F. W. Walther and finding in him a close friend in confessional Lutheranism, Zorn traveled to the United States and served a Missouri Synod congregation in Sheboygan, Wisconsin from 1876–1881. Zorn was twice called to serve Trinity Lutheran Church in St. Louis (Soulard), but declined the call both times. However, in 1881, Zorn accepted a call to a Zion Ev. Lutheran Church in Cleveland, Ohio where he served the final thirty years of his ministry.

Carl Manthey Zorn was a stalwart theologian and a prolific writer. Concordia Historical Institute lists fifty-two books and booklets written by him. Though he is not a household name today, he was well respected by C. F. W. Walther, and following his death, August Pieper wrote over seventy pages in *Theologische Quartalschrift* praising his life's work.

Zorn retired promptly at the age of sixty-five. In his retirement, he gathered around him a group of pastors who sat at his feet to learn about the faith. He also continued writing. This present volume was most certainly penned during his retirement.

Carl Manthey Zorn died on July 12th, 1928 at the age of eighty-two.

THE WRITER INTRODUCES HIMSELF & GREETS THE READER

Romans Chapter 1:1–2

I, the writer of these epistles, who and what am I? I am nothing but a poor echo of the Apostle Paul and of the message he wrote to the Christians in Rome.

Even though I am only that, I know that I can write great and important and divine and soul-saving information to you.

Who was Paul? Paul, also in his office and service, was a slave of Jesus Christ. Indeed, God Himself called him to be an apostle of equal authority with Peter, John and James, and the rest of the Twelve. True, he did not follow Christ at the same time as these, nor did he receive his instructions together at the same time and manner with these, neither did he see the Risen Christ at the same time as they. At that time he was, in fact, an enemy, mocker, and persecutor of the Lord Jesus. But then the Lord Jesus converted him, showed Himself to him as the risen and glorified One, instructed him in all the gospel truths, and finally expressly called him to be His apostle. Therefore, Paul was like the other apostles; specially chosen to preach the gospel of God. And that he did "in words not taught by human wisdom but taught by the Spirit" (1 Cor. 2:13).

So by preaching and by letter, Paul proclaimed the gospel of God: God's Word of grace to the sinful and lost world.

This, His gospel, God has always proclaimed, as long ago as there were sinful and lost people on earth. He proclaimed it to Adam and Eve. He proclaimed it through His prophets, from Moses to Malachi, in His Holy Scriptures which we call the Old Testament. There never has been another gospel than this on earth: namely, this gospel which St. Paul preached and which is being preached among us today. Everything which contradicts or differs from or is added or taken from this gospel at any time or in any respect at all is a lie and a fraud.

However, that proclamation of the gospel which took place before the time of the apostles was a pre-proclamation (proclaimed before it had taken place): a prophesying proclamation. For He, with Whom the gospel is concerned, the very Kernel and Star of God's gospel, He had not as yet appeared at that time. With Whom, namely, does the gospel of the God of all time deal? Concerning Whom does God preach and proclaim through His apostles and prophets?

Letter I
Concerning His Own Son, His Only Son

Romans Chapter 1:3–7

The eternal God, the eternal Father, has an eternal Son, an only begotten Son. This only begotten Son is very God, God from the Father in eternity. He is the one and only God with the Father and the Holy Ghost, that Holy Ghost Who proceeds from the Father and the Son from eternity. And this Son became "flesh," (John 1:14) a human being, in time, in the "fullness of time" (Gal. 4:4). He took on Himself true human nature, taken into His divine person. And, according to His human nature He was begotten out of the seed of David, as it was prophesied of Him. In this manner the Son of God became a human being, just as David was a human being, in very truth. Of course, He was without sin, but He was burdened and affected with the weaknesses and infirmities of our human nature. However, it did not remain like that. After His deepest humiliation in death on the cross, He arose from death, and through His resurrection from the dead, He, the Son of David, was "declared to be the Son of God in power" (1:4). Understand correctly! The Son of David was always the Son of God, but up to this point He had concealed His divine majesty under the form of a servant. Now, however, by His resurrection, the Son of David became the Son of God in power. The humbled One was now so raised up that His human nature now shared in His divine omnipotence fully, constantly, and openly.

God is a Spirit, a Spirit of Holiness, a Spirit of incomparable majesty. According to this Spirit of Holiness, according to this incomparable majesty, you must think of or evaluate the state in which the Son of David now is. And this is Jesus Christ! This is our Lord, Who has redeemed us lost and damned human beings, purchased and won us with His holy, precious blood, and with His innocent suffering and death, that we might be His own in time and in eternity. And, He it is Who now with His divine all-power keeps and protects us as His own for time and eternity. Of this Jesus Christ and of Him alone, all the gospel of God concerns itself for all time and forever.

And through this same Jesus Christ, from this very Jesus Christ, did St. Paul receive the special grace of apostleship (1:5). The special call of the Apostle Paul was this: that he was to establish the obedience of the faith among all Gentiles, that he was to make all Gentiles into believing Christians through the preaching of the gospel of Jesus Christ, that the name Jesus Christ should now also be glorified among the Gentiles.

That was St. Paul. Now, it surely is clear that I, who am no more than a poor mimic of the Apostle Paul and of that which he wrote to the Christians at Rome, can nevertheless and even because of it write things of high and important, godly and soul-saving import and power.

Dear Christian friends, even as the Christians in Rome were almost all Gentiles, so you too are almost all descendants of Gentiles. And just as the Christians in Rome had become "called" ones of Jesus Christ—God made them His own by calling them through the Word and Jesus Christ—so also you have become called ones of Jesus Christ (1:6).

And so I greet all of you (you who are also beloved ones of God and called saints being converted by God's love and Word and separated from the unbelieving world) with that same greeting with which St. Paul greeted the Romans: "Grace to you and peace from God our Father and the Lord Jesus Christ" (1:7). This is no empty human greeting. This is a greeting taken out of God's Word and meant for you. This is a greeting with which God greets you; namely, God the Father, and God the Son—the Lord Jesus—and God the Holy Ghost Who moves and works in and through the Word and wants to make this greeting especially yours. Grasp this greeting by putting your faith in it! Grace shall be with you. The free, undeserved grace that covers all your sins and peace shall be with you. Peace, that tremendous peace of heaven that God is no longer angry with you nor condemns you. And this grace and this peace come to you from God, Who now wants to be your Father, and from Christ Who wants to be your dear Lord. And God the

Father, our Father, speaks His "Amen" to this my greeting, and also our Lord Jesus Christ. And may the Holy Spirit make you likewise speak your "Amen" of faith to it loud and clear!

LETTER II
INTRODUCTION

Chapter 1:8–17

Dear Christians, let me tell you what the Apostle Paul wrote as the introduction to his letter to the Romans.

He says that above everything he thanks his God through Jesus Christ for his Roman Christians, because their faith is spoken of throughout the whole world. Rome, you see, was the world capital, the capital of Gentile power and culture. And, now the gospel had also come to Rome and in Rome there was a Christian congregation. This was spoken of throughout the world with amazement and wonder, with joy among some and with sullen anger among others. Now the name of Christ and the gospel truly did become known in all the world! A deep feeling of thanksgiving and praise to God welled up in Paul's heart because of this. He thanked his God for this, Who had worked it out like this and Who was his dear God and Father, to Whom he belonged as servant and child. And he thanks "my God through Jesus Christ," for it is "through Jesus Christ" that all good things come to us from God, and it is through Christ that all that comes from us to God must go (1:8).

Oh no, what Paul here says was not just empty talk or pious speech. That is why he continues and says that God, Whom he serves in "spirit" (with full and honest heart) in the gospel of His Son, this God was his witness how without ceasing he bears the Roman Christians in mind in this manner just described (1:9).

Then he adds that in all his prayers he also prays, whether it might not finally be possible for him, through God's will, to come to them in Rome. For, he says, he longs to see them that he might share with them some spiritual gift and grace of God through his preaching and encouragement, and that they might be strengthened and fortified in the faith. He then adds in a friendly and modest and yet very truthful manner that he also might be comforted and strengthened by their mutual faith which they both had (1:10–12).

Then he says, he would rather they not be ignorant of the fact that he had often intended to come to visit them, but that he was always prevented from doing so until now. He wanted to visit them in order that he might also produce among them, in Rome, some <u>fruit of faith</u> as was the case among the rest of the Gentiles (1:13). Paul most likely emphasized this so strongly because his enemies were maliciously mocking him and saying that he was afraid to go with his gospel to the "Greeks," or to go to those who prided themselves with the world-famous Greek classic culture. Paul, they twitted, would go with his gospel only to the uneducated and dumb non-Greeks and Barbarians. But, he says, "I am under obligation both to Greeks and to barbarians, both to the wise and to the foolish." (1:14). God had appointed the gospel for all people, for the learned and for the unlearned. Human education and culture do not help anyone to gain the true faith, nor does the lack of them hinder the true faith. Both educated and uneducated people need the gospel to be saved through faith. And Paul was an apostle of the gospel, ordained by God and the Lord Jesus Christ. That is why he owed a debt to the educated and to the uneducated to preach the gospel to them. That is why he says, that as much as depends on him, he is ready to preach the gospel also to them in Rome where such high culture held sway (1:14–15).

From this introduction of the apostle Paul which is not quite yet complete, I, who am writing you these letters take for myself the following.

I, too, thank God for you, since also your faith is spoken of in all the world. You are known and spoken of throughout the world. Why? Because of your faith. In regard to your faith and confession you <u>firmly maintain that Bible-word as God's Word</u>. You hold fast to the old, unadulterated doctrine of Luther, which agrees precisely with God's Word. That, my friends, is nothing short of a miracle in this time of "great falling away." Men stand amazed. Many are overjoyed. Many mock and ridicule you. But, just because of this, "<u>God Word and Luther's doctrine pure</u>" is being made known throughout the whole world. For that I thank God, and I pray God through Jesus Christ, that by His grace He may let me succeed, by means of these letters, to strengthen and establish you and also myself in our common faith, which is being so bitterly spoken against almost everywhere today.

Paul concludes his introduction with these highly significant words, "For I am not ashamed of the gospel, for it is the power of God for salvation to everyone who believes, to the Jew first and also to the Greek. For in it the righteousness of God is revealed from faith for faith, as it is written, 'The righteous shall live by faith'" (1:16–17).

No, Paul was not ashamed or backward at all to come to Rome with the gospel of God concerning His Son, for this gospel is the "God-power" that saves. It provides the saving grace of God in Christ, and it works the faith which takes hold of this saving grace of God in Christ. It is the power of God that saves everyone that believes. All who believe are saved: the Jews, who had this gospel already primarily in the Old Testament, but also the Greeks, the Gentiles, who thought they had wisdom of their own.

For in this gospel (1:17), that righteousness which God accepts is revealed. If a person does not have a righteousness which God accepts, he will be damned. No man has a righteousness that avails before God out of himself, nor knows of one out of himself. At best, he can dream himself into one and deceive himself pitifully. However, in the gospel the righteousness that avails before God "is revealed." Mark well, it is revealed. It is already in existence, already created through the blood and death of Christ and His victorious rising again. Christ has brought this righteousness which avails before God into existence for us. We cannot add a thing to it. God reveals it to us through the gospel. We should now only believe, claim as our own the righteousness which avails before God, prepared for us long ago. So, it comes to us "from faith" (1:17), not from some sort of work of our own. That's the way it is always grasped--"in faith," not by some work somehow. That righteousness is available always and only "from faith," not for any sort of doing or work on our part. Our righteousness which avails before God is already here waiting for us in Christ. All of us are already made righteous before God through Christ. We are informed of this through the gospel. We are only to believe it. Already the prophets in the Old Testament were teaching this. "The righteous shall live by his faith," says Habakkuk 2:4. That means, he who is a righteous one is a righteous one through his faith in the gospel which gives him that righteousness, and so he is saved. This is the way the gospel "is the power of God for salvation to everyone who believes" (1:16).

Should we be ashamed of this old, only eternal, gospel that saves us? Should I be ashamed to write this gospel to you, and to establish you—you who already have it—ever more firmly in it? And should you be ashamed to welcome this gospel ever and again, to cling to it, and to confess it before all the world? Never, no never!

Letter III
The Godless World

Chapter 1:18–32

Now begins the epistle to the Romans.

"The righteous shall live by faith" (1:17b). With these words St. Paul closes his introduction and at the same time announces the main theme of his epistle.

How is it with those who are not righteous before God by faith? How does the godless world fare before God?

With them God is wrathful. Of course, the godless world couldn't care less and isn't concerned about it. But one day it will be very clear to them what it means that God is filled with wrath against them. On the Last Day, God's wrath will be revealed from heaven upon them in a frightening manner (1:18).

Consider for a moment the various kinds of people in this godless world. Godless they are indeed. They have no fear of God in them whatever; neither in their hearts, nor in their lives or conduct. And the truth, the truth that glares into their eyes, cries into their very hearts, which instructs and advises them and tries to better them: this truth they suppress and beat down with their godless wickedness (1:19).

What is this truth? All human beings, bar none, know something about God. That which may be known of God, that the godless also know, for God has showed it unto them. Now, God, as we know, is invisible. However, ever since the world was created, one can and must see and be aware of God's invisible being from the things that are made. God's eternal power and Godhead are clearly seen and recognized in the things He has created. Through His works the invisible God shows clearly that He is here, that He is an almighty God, an eternal God. That He is beyond all measure glorious, great, and holy. God makes this very clear also to the godless so that they are without excuse (1:19–20).

For what excuse might they possibly have, how might they prove that they have not incurred God's wrath? As just demonstrated, they recognized God plainly. Did they then glorify and praise Him as God, the eternal, omnipotent, wonderful, great, and holy God? Did they inquire about Him, fear and respect Him with heart and life? Did they thank Him? They did not. Contrary to better knowledge, they rebuffed, suppressed, and trampled underfoot this truth about God made know to them. Consequently, "they became futile in their thinking" (1:21) and deservedly so, heaping upon themselves guilt upon guilt over and over again. Their thinking and planning, their goals in living centered more and more on temporal things, things that pass away, vanities. Their absurd and silly hearts—which neither wanted to, nor want to listen to and accept as plain, good sense—are now totally darkened. They reached the point where the light of the truth which constantly shines into their hearts out of the works of God no longer has any effect upon them and no longer motivates them toward God at all. They now consider themselves wise, very wise indeed (in their fool's paradise); they condescendingly smile at all recognition of God, reverence toward God, praising or thanking God (1:21–22).

They actually imagine themselves to be the gods of this world and nature. Nature to them is the ultimate and highest quest of all knowledge. And with that they, in truth, turn themselves into unspeakable fools. Isn't that just the way it is? And, the most abominable, the rankest thing which their "futile thinking," (their darkened and unreasonable hearts and insane wisdom) brought forth is that with which the world has been covered for thousands of years. And, what is that? Fallen and godless mankind did indeed have the knowledge of the truth, of the glory of God. That we have clearly seen. But what did they do with that knowledge? They remolded or "exchanged the glory of the immortal God for images resembling mortal man and birds and animals and creeping things" (1:23). God has got to be like these, they say. This is the kind of worship which has flooded the earth for thousands of years.

And for all that they should have an excuse? Which one? Speak up if you know of just one? For what should they not have incurred the wrath and judgment of God? Ah, God gave them truth aplenty to learn, to leave them without excuse whatever. "Now go your way," God says, as it were, to these people already here on earth, "and see for yourselves how far and to what end you will get with your godlessness!" And, as a result, the entire life and doing of the godless people is pure unrighteousness throughout. That is a punishment and a frightful judgment from God—and yet again it is their own fault. God withdraws His hand of blessing from them and abandons them to their hearts' corrupt lusts (1:24).

And to what end did the godless world come by following their own wisdom? First of all, into a horrible condition of uncleanness, endless and boundless whoredom and debauchery. The innocent (in themselves) and sinless sex drives of their natures were turned into nothing but utter uncleanness, lewdness, and shame. Alas, so it is! So, the godless, as a result of God's just punishment and their own fault, come to the point where their own bodies are violated and debased by themselves. A frightfully just punishment indeed! And why? "Because they exchanged the truth about God for a lie and worshiped and served the creature rather than the Creator, who is blessed forever! Amen" (1:25). And, now? Now they dishonor their own God-given bodies. "For this reason God gave them up to dishonorable passions. For their women exchanged natural relations for those that are contrary to nature" (1:26). We won't even go into further detail with this. "And the men likewise gave up natural relations with women and were consumed with passion for one another, men committing shameless acts with men" (1:27). Yes, so they received the wages of their godless and willful error, which were justly well-deserved.

"And since they did not see fit to acknowledge God, God gave them up to a debased mind to do what ought not to be done" (1:28). In their conduct with their neighbor, with their fellowman, they are, as is quite obvious, "filled with all manner of unrighteousness, evil, covetousness, malice. They are full of envy, murder, strife, deceit, maliciousness. They are gossips, slanderers, haters of God, insolent, haughty, boastful, inventors of evil, disobedient to parents, foolish, faithless, heartless, ruthless" (1:29–32).

What a shocking picture of the godless world in only a few lines! But, isn't it strikingly true? Open your eyes and take a good look into the godless world! What is more, it is not like that only among the stark heathen, but actually also in the so-called civilized world. Read this description of the godless world through slowly once again, and then say whether that isn't also true in our world today.

Dear Christians, please mark these two points here. First, this is a portrayal of the entire godless world, of all men who did not become righteous before God by faith. True, this is not to be found in the same measure and in the same degree of open and coarse wickedness and shame. With some, that natural knowledge of God is not so completely subdued. Some, therefore, still practice some degree of outward decency. Some will, in fact, protest against the worst outgrowths of such rottenness and will as a result be laughed at and mocked into silence. Nevertheless, the sprout, the root, the lesser or greater growth, and the fruit of this wickedness is present with all of them, and leads to everlasting death in every case, unless the sinner is made righteous before God by faith in his Savior. Secondly, also we who are Christians and have been justified and born again by faith, see all too clearly that in our old nature we are still afflicted with all those godless drives and propensities. And, this dormant godlessness will all too easily and quickly grow out and destroy us if we do not remain steadfast in our new birth and righteousness by faith. There is but *one* hope for the whole world and for any human being; namely, the righteousness which Jesus Christ has provided, which alone God honors and accepts, and which is received by the individual person by faith produced by the gospel, and which leads without fail to eternal life.

LETTER IV
HYPOCRITES

Chapter 2:1–5

Among the godless servants of sin—who all sin equally against their better knowledge and conscience and so have no excuse in the day of judgment—there are three, distinct classes. The first class consists of those who sin shamelessly without giving it a second thought. They do not try very hard to pretend that what they are doing is good, and in so doing keep up somewhat of a good front. The second and worse class consists of those who even boast of their wickedness and compliment and encourage others when they do such wickedness. Of these two classes I told you in the previous letter. The third and worst class consists of those who judge, condemn, and damn others on account of their sinful living, while at the same time do the very same thing, or even worse. This is the most shocking and hateful sort of hypocrisy. One can hardly believe it possible that there are such people. They are the worst among the godless, and there are many of them. You find these not only among the open and declared unbelievers, but also among nominal Christians who "belong to church."

Let me give you some clear examples of such shameful, almost unbelievable hypocrisy. Some years ago, I knew a rich and respected lady who belonged to a high-class church and to all sorts of social welfare organizations. She was also very active as a member of a temperance society and fought zealously against that oh-so-godless drinking and saloon keeping. She and her society sisters condemned it even if someone would enjoy a social glass of beer. But, she herself, what did she do? She leased one of her houses to a tavern keeper; a second house to another saloon keeper; a third house she rented to a large group of sinful women of the worst sort.

Every month one could see her classy carriage parked in front of this house while she went inside to collect the rent. Other such ladies also very loudly condemn drunkenness and other sins, while they at the same time abort the fruit of their wombs. Yes, they even shamelessly defend such accursed murder, saying that since the unborn fetus belongs to them, they can do with it as they please and that one cannot blame them, etc. Are such murderers to be found only among the upper class women? Aren't there also men who have a lot to say and judge about others and still defend—even promote—such murder of the unborn? How many business people are there who judge and condemn pick-pockets and burglars, while they take advantage of their neighbors in every way possible, rob them and drive them into bankruptcy!

Enough of examples. Now you know who is meant by this third class of sinners. These hypocrites know God's Law and judgment, for they are judging others who do wrong and even do it themselves. They do even worse things than what they condemn in others.

Therefore, O man, you who are hypocritically judging others, you have no excuse whatever, whoever you are. "For in passing judgment on another you condemn yourself, because you, the judge, practice the very same things" (2:1). Yes, even worse things. "We know that the judgment of God rightly falls on those who practice such things. Do you suppose, O man—you who judges those who practice such things and yet do them yourself—that you will escape the judgment of God" (2:2–3)? Do you think, perhaps, that your morality preaching and your judging of others will be reckoned to your credit against your own evil doing? O you hypocrite, the very opposite will happen. You will receive so much greater damnation. Or, what is it that you are thinking? Do you perchance want to make yourself believe that God will spare you on Judgment Day, because He is now still sparing you, and does not let you go to hell right off, as you well deserve it, but rather shows you so much kindness in patience and longsuffering (2:4)?

You godless hypocrite, with such imaginings and lies you are only deceiving yourself. You know better than that! You know all too well and you feel it too, that God with His kindness leads you to repentance. But you do not want to know, nor understand that. You purposely want to misunderstand. You do not want to let yourself be led to repentance. You are fighting God off. You are willfully shaking off the impression that God's kindness is making on you. And, so, you are actually despising the riches of God's grace and patience and longsuffering. Instead of repenting and allowing yourself to be rescued, you with your hard and impenitent heart are actually heaping up for yourself the vengeance and wrath that will descend upon you on the day of wrath and revelation of the righteous judgment of God (2:5).

No, no, I don't mean any of you who are God's dear children with these hard words. I mean the godless hypocrite, who judges others because of their sin and does the very same himself. But, take the warning to heart! Keep yourselves in the righteousness of God, in the righteousness by faith that alone proves valid before God. Remain in the "new birth" of God which is your faith! Only in doing that will you be kept safe from that lurking danger. Remember, that sort of evil thing still remains in our old sinful nature as well, and those who fall away from the faith become the worst of unbelievers, like those just described. Think of King David, how he flared up in anger against the man of whom Nathan told him, and offhand condemned him to death (2 Sam. 12:5), and see what he himself had done! And, how hardened in sin he was for nearly a whole year! Only after God's rescuing grace through the, "You are the man!" (2 Sam. 12:7) flung him to the ground, and then through "The Lord also has put away your sin" (2 Sam. 12:13), put him back on his feet and brought him back to the righteousness of faith and to the new birth again. Only after that did David become a different man and was rescued from his folly.

There is no other help for us in our desperate condition, either, except the righteousness that avails before God which becomes our own by faith.

Letter V
The Judgment

Chapter 2:6–16

The godless world which is not righteous by faith in God's sight is guilty before God because of its unrighteousness and has nothing that it could offer as an excuse. Therefore, it is under God's judgment. This we have seen. Let us now consider the judgment: the great final judgment.

To begin with, for us Christians it is beyond all doubt that God will judge according to the gospel; namely, according to faith or unbelief. For "God so loved the world, that he gave his only Son, that whoever believes in him should not perish but have eternal life." (John 3:16). And, "Whoever believes and is baptized will be saved, but whoever does not believe will be condemned" (Mark 16:16). All Scripture teaches that unanimously. The prophets, Christ himself, and the apostles all teach that. To this we hold fast with total confidence.

But, just as unanimously, all Scripture: the prophets, Christ, and the apostles also teach that God will judge according to works. Therefore, St. Paul writes to the Romans, that God on Judgment Day, "will render to each one according to his works" (2:6).

God help us, what is that? Do the Scriptures, the prophets, Christ, and the apostles contradict themselves? Have we poor sinners misplaced our confidence that we are saved by grace? Far from it! But, how is it? It's like this: on Judgment Day, God will, indeed, judge according to faith or unbelief; but, He will publicly demonstrate by the works of men, who has been a believer or an unbeliever. Believers, you see, no longer are slaves of sin, but serve God with good works; and, that they do out of love to their gracious God, by the power of the Holy Spirit, even though, of course, very imperfectly. The unbelievers are constantly serving sin and do not produce even one genuinely good work out of love to God and by the Holy Spirit, for they hate God and will have nothing of the Holy Spirit. God will openly demonstrate for all concerned who has faith and who has no faith. In this sense, God "will render to each one according to his works" (2:6). However, "Whoever believes and is baptized will be saved, but whoever does not believe will be condemned" (Mark 16:16). That stands firm.

Now, do you understand what St. Paul means when he says that God, "will render to each one according to his works" (2:6)?

First, there are the believers, the poor sinners who were made righteous before God by faith in Christ. These continue in the good Christian life, stir themselves up continually to live as Christians should live, strive to gain eternal life. That is an evidence of their faith. According to this, God will deal with them on Judgment Day, and will give them heavenly glory and the pure gifts of everlasting life in eternal existence. God has—as we know—promised such things to faith, and in this manner God will repay even the few, paltry works of believers. But—and mark this well—He will repay out of overwhelming grace, and not because they earned or merited it (2:7).

Then, there are the godless, the unbelievers, who refuse to become righteous before God by faith. These are self-willed, stubborn, and refuse to be led. They will not listen to the truth, by which God leads them from evil to the right way.

They insist on obeying and serving sin and unrighteousness. That attitude is evidence and proof of their unbelief. On Judgment Day, God will deal with them according to this unbelief. He will give them His wrath and anger to endure. In this manner, He will punish their evil works as they deserve it (2:8).

Furthermore, God will send hopeless desperation and anguish into the soul of every man who does evil even though he clearly knows better. And, this God will do primarily to the Jews, who had His Law and covenant from of old, but transgressed it. Also to the Gentiles, who against better knowledge will serve sin. Most of all, however, God will do this to fallen-away and hypocritical Christians, who have the fullest light of God's truth, but despise it. "But glory and honor" and that precious, sweet peace of eternal salvation God will give to each one, who, by faith in Jesus Christ does what is good, primarily the Jew as the true member of the old church of God, and also the Gentile, who became a true member of the church (2:9–10).

For, listen and mark it well, "God shows no partiality" (2:11). As many as had been Gentiles and as such did not have the written Law of the Ten Commandments, but had sinned, they will be lost also without this Law. And, as many as had been Jews and so had the written Law of Ten Commandments and sinned against it, they will through this same Law be judged and condemned (2:12). This is above all true with those who had enjoyed the blessings of the Christian Church, and yet sinned in spite of it all. "For it is not the hearers of the law who are righteous before God" (2:13), but those as before described, who through faith in Christ become doers of the Law, who will be publicly justified by God on Judgment Day.

You say, perhaps: That I see clearly. But one thing only is not clear to me. By what will the Gentiles who sinned be judged if they did not even have the written Law of Ten Commandments? How can one, therefore, say that they sinned against their better knowledge? True! But, did you forget what I pointed out already in Letter III? But, listen further.

It happens often, without a doubt, that Gentiles who do not have the written Law, do by nature the commandments of the divine Law. What I mean is this, Gentiles—without knowing about the written Law—avoid and shun many coarse and shameful vices forbidden in the divine Law and are very intent in many ways to practice a respectful and decent lifestyle. They do it out of an indwelling natural compulsion or drive. They, even though they have no knowledge of the written Law, are a law unto themselves. Of course, what they do real well in one respect, that they do not at all well in the other; and, in any case, it is at best a mere superficial do-good performance. Yet, what do the Gentiles show and prove by it all (2:14)?

They show the work of the Law written in their hearts, that God has given them, into their inner nature, a knowledge of His Law. Right? Indeed, God has written His Law into the hearts of men. And such writing in the heart which shows the works of the Law is not entirely erased in the Gentiles, not even among the coarsest of them. Conscience, which all Gentiles have, makes that clear. All Gentiles have a conscience, an inner awareness, and a knowledge of this Law of God written into their hearts. This conscience also testifies concerning this Law of God in their hearts. The thoughts of the Gentiles speak with each other, accusing or else excusing somewhat like: "Ah, yes, here I really sinned frightfully; yes, but it isn't quite as bad as all that. It happened so quickly, you see. I was tricked into it, you see." Or, like this perhaps: "This I dare not do; that's bad, but that—oh well, that's all right" (2:15).

Now doesn't that clearly show that God's Law is written into their hearts and that they are also aware of the fact that God is right there with them as Lawgiver and Judge? And, isn't it also clear now by what the Gentiles are being judged, even though they do not have the written Law, the Ten Commandments? Furthermore, you will see also how one can honestly say that they sin against their better knowledge. They do know better. Their conscience and inner knowledge of the divine Law will rise up against them on the Day of Judgment as accuser and, at the same time, as witness that they sinned in spite of it all. They will have no excuse whatever.

And, now hear this! In all truth and in utter finality this is the way it is on Judgment Day: "God judges the secrets of men" (2:16). 'The secrets of men' is their faith or unbelief in their hearts. And so, God will judge "according to my Gospel" he who believes will be saved; he who does not believe will be damned (2:16). "By Christ Jesus," God will judge. God will judge by our good and beloved Savior, Who would so gladly save us all. In Him put your faith! Then be completely at peace with your God! (2:16).

LETTER VI
THE JEWS

Chapter 2:17–29

Dear Christians, may I remind you briefly of what I have written to you up until now out of the Epistle to the Romans? And may I point out to you how this letter is related to the previous letters? I'm sure it will serve to a better understanding.

The godless world, which is not by faith righteous before God, stands guilty before God. It has nothing it can offer to God as an excuse and thus stands condemned in God's presence. This is true especially of those who hypocritically condemn others while doing the same thing. And the judgment of God will come upon every godless one without respect of persons, regardless of whether he be Gentile, Jew, or "Christian." This I have pointed out in the previous three letters. However, since I, in the previous letters, spoke especially about the Gentiles, now I want to speak especially of the Jews.

When I say that I want to speak of the Jews, I mean particularly those Jews of all times as well as of our day who do not believe in Jesus Christ as the only Savior and are therefore not righteous before God. That, I believe, is self-evident. One thing more: I wish to speak in particular of those Jews, who really want to be Jews, and not of such who have thrown everything away and have so become just godless Gentiles. Of these last mentioned, the same is true what was said of the Gentiles.

Still one thing more: I believe it is good and necessary that it be clearly shown (from God's Word) how we are to think of and consider the Jews. As you know, it is often asked, "How is it with the Jews? Will they be saved, or will they be condemned?" Such questions obviously betray a lot of spiritual misunderstanding. But they do arise; therefore, it is good and necessary to hear the answer to these questions from God's Word.

Now, the Jews, the real Jews, take pride in their name. They are proud to be Jews, that sort of ancient people that has its roots in Abraham, Isaac, and Israel, and that takes its name from Judah. They are, indeed, a people to be marveled at. And, they look down proudly on other nationalities as Gentiles. That whereon they depend for support is that God has given them His Law and revealed Himself to them on Mt. Sinai and through the writings of the prophets, before all other peoples of the earth. This is, in fact, true. So they boast themselves of God (2:17).

And since they are being instructed by the writings of the Old Testament, they are acquainted with God's will, and test and judge with that the difference between what is right and wrong. That being the case, they confidently present themselves as leaders of the blind, light to those in darkness, as instructors of the foolish, as a teacher of babes, such as which they consider all other people. "You see," they say, "we have our Law and Holy Scriptures, the right form and character, the right revelation and presentation of knowledge and truth." This is, in fact, the truth. But, they who teach others do not teach themselves. Yes, mark it well, dear reader, what I say. They who teach others don't teach themselves. They preach that one should not steal, and they steal (2:18–21).

Their own prophets already in ancient pre-Christian times openly accused them of screaming injustices in trade and commerce. It isn't really necessary that I waste a good many words to show that the Jews are even today yet among the real, true, and original swindlers. They say one should not commit adultery, and they commit adultery (2:22). I must say, that I always thought that in this respect the Jews were better than the Gentiles. But, I was wrong, for their own prophets in ancient pre-Christian days accused them of this sin. Their own non-biblical writings, the so-called Talmud, etc., do the same. One knows of a lot of such uncleanness among them. They are an exceptionally pleasure-seeking race. They, furthermore, abhor idols with a vengeance, yet they are not concerned about God, but rob Him of what is His: His honor and the service He deserves. In short, they boast before all nations that they have the Law of God, while through breaking the Law they dishonor God (2:23). Their own prophets in ancient, pre-

Christian times already reproached them and threw it into their teeth that on their account "the name of God is blasphemed among the Gentiles" (2:24), as written in the Old Testament. It has always been like that and still is today. Well, what must come of all this? Isn't it plain that the Jews, even less than the Gentiles, will escape the wrath and judgment of God? The answer is clear, of course! It is precisely their Law which they have and know, and of which they boast, that will judge and condemn them before all the Gentiles. It's frightful! But, don't you see it yourself? The only ones who will stand even guiltier in God's judgment than the Jews are the hypocrites among the Christians, who boast of the Christian name and, perhaps, also of the pure doctrine and yet with it all sin openly against God's Law, giving cause and occasion for Gentiles and unbelievers to mock and blaspheme God and His Word, Christianity, and the Christian faith.

But, we haven't quite finished with the Jews as yet. Their real steel fortress in which they put their trust is the circumcision. They boast and brag that they are circumcised. They mean that, because they are circumcised, they will not be lost but will be saved. Well, what is—or better yet—what was the circumcision? It was the first God-ordained sacrament given to Abraham and his seed. He who was circumcised was through it made a member of the chosen people of God. Through it God offered, gave, and sealed to him, the circumcised one, every grace and blessing which God had solemnly promised to His people in Christ, the Messiah—do you hear? In Christ. The circumcised one was, therefore, to believe the Word of God about the Christ. He was to gratefully accept the grace and blessings offered to him in circumcision for the sake of the coming Christ, and after that to prove the genuineness of his faith by doing God's will as stated in the Law of God. That is the circumcision of which the Jews boast and brag. So, as you can see, circumcision did have a great, eternal, and blessed gift to give—if the one circumcised, by faith in Christ, kept the Law as God's dear child should. However, if he was a godless and unbelieving breaker of the law, he thereby threw away the blessings of the circumcision and his circumcision became uncircumcision. See what I mean? That's the way it was in the Old Testament with most of the Jews.

Of what do the Jews of today want to boast concerning the circumcision and so elevate themselves above all other people? Do they believe in Christ and do they prove their faith by keeping the Law? They do not. We saw just a bit ago how grossly they despise God's Word of grace and transgress His Law.

Their circumcision has become uncircumcision. Uncircumcised Gentiles now believe in Christ, and prove their faith through sincere and heartfelt, even though imperfect, keeping of the commandments of the Law, and so their uncircumcision becomes circumcision. I think you understand, don't you? The believing Gentiles are not the people of God and have all the graces and blessings that were promised to the Jews and given to them by the circumcision. Those by nature uncircumcised, but now believing Gentiles, who prove their faith through fulfilling the Law, will in God's eyes judge the Jews, who outwardly have the letter of the Law and the circumcision, but are faithless and godless transgressors of the Law (2:25–27).

For in true reality he is not a Jew who is one only outwardly. Neither is that a circumcision which is one outwardly, that is, in the flesh only. But he is a true Jew, and a member of the true people of God, who in the hidden depths of his heart by faith in Christ is a Jew like Abraham, Moses, David, Peter, Paul, or also like Mary Magdalene and the malefactor on the cross and thousands of others. And he whose flesh is circumcised not only according to the outward letter, but has his heart circumcised by faith worked by the Holy Spirit (so that he now willingly and gladly renounces sin and serves God) that one is truly circumcised and his praise is not a vain and empty self-praise of mere men, but his praise is of God (2:29).

I would beg you, dear reader, to apply what has been said about the circumcision of the Jews, to your baptism. That would indeed be a very salutary exercise. Do it in answer to the question, "When does baptism benefit those who are baptized?"

LETTER VII
EVERY MAN IS GUILTY BEFORE GOD

Chapter 3:1–8

So, we have seen that the Jews, no less than the Gentiles (yes, even more so), stand guilty before God and under the curse of the Law.

But, if that is true, the questions arise: "Then what advantage has the Jew? Or what is the value of circumcision?" (3:1).

To these questions comes the answer: The advantage of the Jews and the benefit of circumcision is manifold in every respect. It consists, primarily, in this: that God entrusted His Word to them. In the Old Testament Scriptures they had the revelations of God. These gave them the right and full understanding of God's Law. And more, much more. In these divine revelations they had the gracious promises of God concerning Christ, the Savior, who was to be born among them and would complete His gracious work in their very midst. Surely, this is an advantage and benefit! Of course, the great majority of the Jews treated His precious gift very badly and faithlessly. They were godless and faithless. They despised God's gracious Word and broke word and faith with God. I am now speaking of the times of the Old Testament. What if some were unfaithful? Will their unfaithfulness make God unfaithful? Never! God kept His Word as promised. God let them keep His Law and His promises. God continuously taught, warned, chastised, and threatened them with His Law. God enticed and coaxed them constantly in the most gracious and friendly ways possible through His many precious promises until He finally fulfilled them all to the last in the appearance of Christ the Messiah. Indeed, God truly gave the Jews a great advantage over the Gentiles. He offered them great benefits in this: that He through circumcision made them His very own people (3:2).

But since the great majority of the Jews flung away this advantage and benefit we can ask, "In spite of all this: why, and for what reason, and for what purpose did God still keep faith with them?" To this question I find a two-fold answer. First, God kept His Word to the Jews despite all because there were still only "some" that were faithless, but not all. God still wanted to keep His promise true to these few, right? Second, God remained true to the faithless Jews despite everything, in order that He finally, on Judgment Day, would stand before the whole world as the Truthful One, Who stood by His Word. In contrast, the Jews would be exposed all the more distinctly and clearly as liars and lovers of the lie, as enemies of the divine truth, and as children of the devil—the arch enemy of the truth. On Judgment Day, it shall be revealed clear and plain how just and righteous God is when He pronounces His flaming words of damnation against the Jews. Triumphantly, God will stand in His untouchable and unreproachable righteousness when He judges the faithless traitors. For this reason, God kept His Word to the perfidious Jews and allowed them to keep their great advantage through the years.

Yes, and God kept His Word to each and every human being in order that He would be true and all human beings would stand there as liars, lovers of the lie, enemies of truth, and as children of the devil. This He did so that He will be righteous in His words of condemnation and victorious in His judgment when He will be attacked because of His judging (3:4).

We have seen in detail how God did not leave Himself without witness also to the Gentiles, so that they would have no excuse whatever on Judgment Day. Even we who are Christians, whom God by His rich grace and Spirit has made to be true to Himself, and who by faith in Christ will be saved—even we will have to confess on the Day of Judgment, "Dear God, it is all because of Your grace; You alone are righteous and true; we are sinners and unjust. You have remained true to us throughout. We have deserved nothing but Your wrath and condemnation. You alone have rescued us by Your grace and truth. We, left to ourselves alone, are lost children of lies and unfaithfulness."

In this manner God wants to make His righteousness stand out in bold relief by our unrighteousness. Through our lies He will glorify His truthfulness. God will make our unrighteousness and perfidy serve Him by making His righteousness and faithfulness shine forth all the more gloriously. This, dear reader, this we must try our best to consider and understand real well. Psalm 51:4 says it like this: "Against you, you only, have I sinned and done what is evil in your sight, so that you may be justified in your words and blameless in your judgment." (All this, so that God might be acclaimed as altogether just when He speaks in condemning us and be clear when He judges. That is, that He might be seen by all as pure of all fault when He judges us.) That is exactly as it is.

But now, I want to let human reason ask a question. Namely, "But if our unrighteousness serves to show the righteousness of God," as was pointed out, "what shall we say?" (3:5). We certainly shall not say that God is unjust in that He threatens us with His wrath on account of our unrighteousness, shall we? You see, our poor reason would like to think that God would not be altogether just if He would use our unrighteousness to show forth and glorify His own righteousness, when He would enter into judgment against us on account of this our unrighteousness. Well, what shall we answer to this question of human reason? Simply, and in brief, this: "God forbid that God could in any respect be unjust." For then how shall God judge the world? It is an absolutely anti-Scriptural and God-insulting folly to think that the very source and fountain of all justice could in any respect be unjust (3:5–6). This circumstance, that God nevertheless judges us as sinners, despite the fact that our unrighteousness proves Him righteous, and despite the fact that God's truthfulness is established and exalted by our perfidy—this circumstance demonstrates, on the contrary, God's unimpeachable righteousness. For, it surely would be proof positive of unrighteousness and corruption if a judge should say to a lawbreaker, "Since I have profited from your evil deeds, I will not punish you." And the criminal would then say, "I will commit crimes in order that good might come of it for the judge." But God is not such an unrighteous judge (3:7).

So, then, this is the way we should think and speak: "If God's truthfulness were magnified through our perfidy to His glory, why then are we still being judged as sinners?" Answer: "Because God is beyond all doubt righteous and would justly have to condemn us even more." It is a lie and a blasphemy for us to say when unbelievers mock us, "Since God is glorified through our sinning (for in forgiving all our sins, God's great grace surely stands out and His greatness shows itself most wonderfully in this, that He makes even some good grow out of our sinning), therefore, we will go right on sinning all out." Never! Such a hell-born conclusion we shall most certainly not draw from this (3:8).

Now then, what have we learned today, dear reader? We have learned that all human beings are guilty before God and have deserved His just punishment. This stands sure. It stands firm and sure even more, because God did not permit the perfidy of human beings to destroy His truth and faithfulness. And it remains true, even though God lets the sins of men serve to glorify Him.

Dear Christians, surely nothing can help us sinners except the righteousness which alone avails before God and is given as a free gift to faith!

Letter VIII
Utterances of God Which Accuse Mankind

Chapter 3:9–20

Well, then. What is the ultimate result of what we have said till now? The Jews, whom God has given such a great advantage over the Gentiles, have they finally the best of it? Are they finally more important to God than the Gentiles? Absolutely not! For in the foregoing letters it surely was conclusively proven that Jews and Gentiles, and all human beings are equally sinful, that sin lies on all like a heavy, inexcusable debt. And since these letters taken out of the Epistle to the Romans are God's Word, then what has been said is certainly divinely true.

But God has already from ancient times (in the Old Testament) pronounced the same judgment on all men. I will now bring such ancient divine utterances which show this in astonishing clarity.

The Apostle Paul cites the mouth of the royal prophet David, by whom the Lord Jehovah pronounces this judgment from heaven on the children of men, "None is righteous, no, not one; no one understands; no one seeks for God. All have turned aside; together they have become worthless; no one does good, not even one" (3:10b–12). And more: "Their throat is an open grave; they use their tongues to deceive. The venom of asps is under their lips. Their mouth is full of curses and bitterness" (3:13–14). See also Isaiah 59:7–8. And lastly, God speaks through David, "There is no fear of God before their eyes" (3:18). Godless, without fear of God and sense of reverence are all men, and out of that comes all the evil they do.

This is a frightful divine judgment over all and every man. And God knows whereof He speaks. He does not lie nor exaggerate.

And, dear friend, I who write this know from personal experience that God speaks the truth. I see all this clearly and distinctly in myself. I am, thanks to God, a Christian. But, I see all this without exception in my old Adam, my old nature.

But, we do not want to play hide-and-seek. We want to bring to light a thought that wanted to sneak into our minds before already, namely this, "Human beings are portrayed as too frightfully bad. There are millions, to be sure, that are that bad. But, there are also among unbelievers a good number who are not all that bad."

So, there he stands, that thought, in the light. He wanted to rebel secretly against God's Word. What to do with him?

Hear a parable! See, a great wide field, filled every inch with weeds. Some are high and overripe, scattering their evil seed. Some are still in blossom and don't look so bad at all. Still some others are very small and seems very cute and innocent. But, it's all the same weed. All of it will in time grow to the same ripeness. And, if one would want to characterize this weed correctly, one would first describe its evil sort or kind and secondly, its evil fruit, regardless of size or age or stage of the plant. Need I explain this parable? The world is the field, the weeds are the people, sin-corrupted human beings. Some of us are obviously fully ripe in evil doing. Others not far from it, but do not show as much. Still others are still sprouting and developing in their evil nature and seem quite innocent, but all have the same sinful and corrupt nature. And all, given time and opportunity, will become fully mature in wickedness, unless they are born again by God's Word and Spirit and are made God's dear children and righteous by faith. And should one now want to correctly characterize these human beings, one must describe them first according to their evil kind or sort and second, according to their evil fruits, which their evil kind naturally brings forth. With all this, one dare not take into account the fact that not every person has come to the same stage of ripeness, and that not everyone so obviously displays the poisonous fruits of their evil nature, like some savages or some reprobates in our civilized world. So, God describes and faults all mankind without exception (3:10–19).

Now what happens to that sneaky thought? Ridiculous, isn't it?

Here is another observation, dear reader, about the Law and the Jews and all who have and know it. We know very well, of course, that whatever the Law says and commands it says especially to those who are under the Law. Naturally! But, do you know what

God's design and purpose are with the Law? Precisely this: "that every mouth may be stopped"—can't bring one single excuse anymore—"and the whole world may be held accountable before God," not only the Gentiles and those who grew up without the Law, but also especially the Jews and all who have and know it (3:19).

Yes, but how will that happen to all who are under the Law? Because then it will be clear as day that "no human being" does or can possibly do what the Law demands, and that no human being can be justified before God by doing the things demanded by the Law, "since through the Law comes knowledge of sin" (3:20). The clearer one understands the Law, the clearer it will become to him that he does not keep nor is able to keep the Law, that he is not righteous before God, that he has to remain speechless and is totally guilty before God. Precisely, the Law shows us our desperate corruption, damns our good works, our words, our thoughts, our desires, lights up our inmost heart, throws blinding light upon our most deeply ingrained wickedness and godlessness, makes it clear that every excuse, every objection, every attempt to talk oneself out of it, is in vain. Yes, it incriminates us all the more before the holy and righteous God. And, whoever refuses to let his mouth be stopped and refuses to confess himself guilty before God by the Law, he will have it done to him by the same Law on Judgment Day without fail (3:20).

With this observation, dear reader, we have returned to the beginning of this letter, where it was said that the Jews were not preferred in any manner to others despite the great advantage they had of the Gentiles, and that Jews and Gentiles and all people are altogether in equal measure under sin, which lies like a heavy, inexcusable debt on all men alike. Let this truth sink deeply into your heart, dear Christian, and hold on tight to the righteousness by faith. This is your only but most certain help and hope.

LETTER IX
THE RIGHTEOUSNESS THAT FULLY MEETS GOD'S REQUIREMENTS

Romans 3:21–26

My dear Christians! I have written eight letters to you out of the Epistle to the Romans. In these I have put before you what St. Paul writes and teaches in the first chief part of his Epistle to the Romans; namely, that all human beings without distinction are sinners, guilty before God, without excuse, and condemned. That is God's Word. And what it says and means is frightful beyond measure.

Now we come to the second and chief part of the Epistle to the Romans, which is truly the chief part of the whole epistle. This one Paul begins with the words: "But now."

Yes, there is a "But now," that successfully challenges all the terrors of our doom, sets us free, and saves us. Now our mouths shall be made happy and we shall be made young as eagles so that we shall rise up to God, fly into His arms, and filled with ecstasy call Him "Abba, dear Father!" And you, Christians, already know this. In every letter so far, especially in the second, this precious "But now" is mentioned. Now, however, I want to place before your very souls what this "But now" really means.

For us—who have in ourselves absolutely no righteousness whatever that avails before God and with which we can stand before God, who have absolutely nothing but unrighteousness, sin, guilt, and damnation—there is now, despite everything, a righteousness which fully meets God's requirements, which the Most High fully accepts, and with which we shall be able to stand before God, and be found righteous and blessed. This righteousness is ready and waiting for us here and now. Nothing, no nothing whatsoever needs to be added to it, least of all from us.

But, this righteousness is to us and our nature, totally strange, totally unknown, totally undiscoverable, and completely beyond our understanding. It is revealed to us by God, and made known through the gospel. Already through "the Law and the prophets," that is through the Old Testament Scripture, this righteousness is attested and declared. This righteousness is foreshadowed by the entire Old Testament worship. It is typified and placed before us. Yes, indeed, in the Old Testament there was also gospel which revealed this righteousness. This righteousness is revealed to us by God without and apart from the Law having anything to add to it. The Law is not even mentioned by it, has nothing to do with it, nothing whatsoever. When we are told of this righteousness out of the gospel, we are not even to think of the Law, need not even be concerned about the Law. The Law has no right whatsoever to interrupt, has no business whatsoever to make demands, threats, curses. The Law, in fact, has here lost all its demanding and damning power and validity. What kind of righteousness indeed might this be?

Listen well and take note! Every word is important. It is the righteousness before God, which comes by and with the faith in Jesus Christ. Jesus Christ is made righteousness for us by God. Jesus Christ, according to God's gracious counsel and will as our Substitute or Proxy procured for us the righteousness which avails before God—with which we stand before God. So then, we are not our own righteousness; no, Jesus Christ is our righteousness. And Jesus Christ with His righteousness which He procured for us is being revealed to us, proclaimed, offered, pressed upon us, and given to us. And we are simply to accept Jesus Christ with His righteousness, believe in Him, trustingly make Him our own. Nothing else, nothing. Then we have Him and His righteousness which is for us. Then we have the righteousness that avails before God, with which we stand before God. In this manner the righteousness is brought by us before God, through faith in Christ Jesus. This righteousness is meant by God for all. Yes, for all, that they simply accept the same and believe it. In this way, Christ's righteousness comes upon all who believe, simply believe: like a mighty, heavenly divine blessing of grace. What a miracle! What wondrous grace, experienced by all who believe! For here there is no difference; they, the believers, one and all are sinners and are lacking the praise that God gives, lacking one and all, all worth and worthiness in God's sight, and yet are justified before God, are made righteous by God, pronounced righteous, declared righteous. How so? In what way? On what grounds? This I will now explain again, but this time in greater detail, more exactly, and more intensely and penetratingly (3:23).

We become righteous in God's sight without deserving it, altogether free, Scot free. God gives us the righteousness as a totally undeserved gift. All that we have, as we well know, is sin and guilt. Therefore, by God's totally free grace, to which we in no way whatever can lay claim, we become righteous before God.

In this grace God has sent His Son, our Lord Jesus Christ. He came to rescue us guilty and condemned sinners as our Substitute, took on Himself our guilt and punishment, redeemed us, bought us free from all we deserved. In this manner we were made righteous before God through the redemption, the purchase of Jesus Christ.

And this Jesus Christ God has set before us and the whole world, before our very eyes, through the Gospel, in order that we should believe in Him, grasp Him and that righteousness given to us in Him by faith, and have it all together with Him as our very own possession, and so become righteous before God.

Jesus Christ is the true Mercy Seat (Ex. 25:17–22), the Lid of Atonement. How so? What is that? In the Old Testament there was first the Tabernacle and then the Temple, the holy place of God's people. Here in the holy place behind the curtain was the Holy of Holies. In the Holy of Holies stood the Ark of the Covenant (Lev. 16:2) with the tables of the Law. Upon this Ark of the Covenant was a cover or lid, the Lid of Atonement or Mercy Seat as it is called. On the Mercy Seat stood two golden cherubim (angels), and between their extended wings was the *shechinah* (the Dwelling), by which the Lord made His presence known. Once each year, on the Great Day of Atonement, the high priest brought a sacrifice of blood into it, in order to pay for the sin and debt of the whole people of Israel and so to reconcile with God. With the blood of the sacrifice he went behind the curtain into the Holy of Holies and sprinkled the Mercy Seat with it. So then, according to God's ordinance and command and in the immediate presence of God, the high priest stroked the blood of reconciliation and atonement on the lid—under which laid the Law which condemned the people. In this manner, this lid became the Lid of Atonement, a Mercy Seat, upon which the now reconciled God was enthroned. All this, however, was only a type or foreshadowing of Jesus Christ. Jesus Christ is the true High Priest, the true Sacrifice, and the true Lid of Atonement or Mercy Seat in His blood. He covers the Law before God's eyes so that it no longer can demand anything from us anymore or condemn us, for Christ has paid our debt through His blood; He has reconciled God to us, has made us righteous in the sight of God. For, when our debt is paid and when God is reconciled to us, then are we righteous before God. And God has presented Him, this Jesus Christ, to us in the gospel or "Lid of Atonement in His blood," that we should believe in Him and that we, through such faith, should grasp and hold the righteousness He has given us.

But is not God righteous? Does He not punish sin? Indeed, He does. He is Righteousness itself. God would no sooner surrender His righteousness than He would surrender Himself. Where then was that righteousness of God in all the centuries before Christ, when He did not punish those heaven-defying sins of the people, at least not in this life nor as fully deserved, but overlooked them, as it were? Where, after all, is this righteousness of God, when He forgives sin and declares the sinners righteous? Here is the answer. God has punished the sins of all times and of all human beings fully and completely and with the most severe justice on Christ, our Substitute, our Stand-In. And when He places before us and presents to us Christ as a Lid of Atonement in His blood, He demonstrates clearly that He surely does hold fast to His policy of just punishment. Those many sins committed in the many centuries in the Old Testament which God seemingly overlooked, He overlooked only in view of the full completion and proof of His righteousness and justice in Christ on Calvary in the fullness of time. For God certainly did finally and fully punish all sins in Christ, and in presenting Christ to us as Lid of Atonement in His blood, God furthermore demonstrates and wants to demonstrate that *He* remains fully righteous also when He forgives sin and declares the sinners righteous. He has punished Christ in the sinners' stead and place.

In conclusion, God presented Christ to faith as the Lid of Atonement and Mercy Seat in His blood, in order that He (i.e.,

God) might remain righteous and declare righteous that person who has faith in Christ.

So, then, the righteousness that avails before God is: (1) a dearly purchased one—given to us by grace, and (2) a perfectly flawless one, that is, a completely unimpeachable and untouchable one. This righteousness is unimpeachable and untouchable equally for us who receive it, as well as in God's sight, Who gives it to us as an outright gift.

And this one, O Christians, this righteousness, grasp it and cling to it in faith! He who will not do this, upon him God's judgment must descend!

Letter X
The Faith Which Justifies before God

Romans 3:27–31

We human beings love to boast of ourselves. It's a part of the corruptions of our entire human nature. Even the guiltiest criminal lout wants to know something about himself to boast of. Even he who has received the most amazing and purest grace searches for something which might make him more worthy than others of such grace (3:27). But, how is it when we, with the Spirit's leading, rightly consider and study this Christian truth in Holy Scripture? Where then is such boasting? It is excluded. How so? According to what law? I mean, by what rule or principle of judgment is boasting locked out? According to the rule of works? Is such boasting excluded if one is judged by God's Law and by the works demanded by it? No, not then. For, as far as works are concerned, a person has in addition to the bad also some good, and one person is perhaps less worthless or even more so than another. So, you see, boasting always enters in again. Well then, according to what rule or judging principle or order is boasting excluded? According to that of faith. For here is our banner, our high-flying standard that boldly displays the shortest yet most striking confession of Christian truth. That is, our glorious banner woven by the Holy Spirit Himself out of God's own Holy Gospel, proclaiming, "For we hold that one is justified by faith apart from works of the law" (3:28).

This apostolic dictum of God's Word we shall now try to fully understand. Everything depends upon this, that a person is righteous before God, that we are declared righteous, and judged as righteous by God. Thus, we are forced to this conclusion which is our overpowering conviction forced upon us by the Holy Spirit, that a man, a person whoever he may be, is made righteous by faith without the deeds of the Law.

A person becomes righteous before God, is justified, by faith alone. By what faith? By the faith in Jesus Christ. In ourselves we have no righteousness at all with which we can stand before God—none whatsoever. Furthermore, even if we had all eternity, we could *still* produce no righteousness out of ourselves. But, Jesus Christ is made for us Righteousness by God. He is the true Mercy Seat in His blood. It is as such that He is set before us by God through the gospel. "There, there is your righteousness," says God to us, "that righteousness is My gift to you." Now, what is there left for us to do? Nothing. We are simply to accept what God says, receive what God gives, and trustingly rely on what God tells us—and gives to us—in a word, "believe." Then we have the righteousness that God accepts, that counts with God. Then we are justified. That is the Christian truth. We become righteous before God by faith alone. Consequently, where is boasting then? It is excluded, out!

A man is made just, is justified before God "apart from works of the law," by faith alone (3:28). By the works of the Law, by the works which the Law demands, we cannot become righteous before God, because we cannot do them. We can never do them in such a manner that we can become righteous before God by them. But, thank God, we are made righteous before God without the works of the Law, by faith alone. Without even one solitary work of the Law on our part of any kind, alone by faith, we are justified. If we had to produce even only one, single work of the Law of our own selves, we would be lost, because we cannot produce one, solitary work of such quality whatever it may be, with which we can hope to stand before God. We become righteous before God by faith alone, without the works of the Law, without the works required of us by the second table, that is, without love to the neighbor. Our love to our neighbor shows itself in this, that we from the heart sincerely honor our parents and superiors, that we do not kill, do not commit adultery, do not steal, do not bear false witness, do not covet anything which belongs to our fellowman, but from the heart wish and do him only well. We become righteous before God also without the works the Law requires of us in the first table, namely without fear, love, or trust to God, without keeping and regarding His name and Word holy. We become righteous before God without the works of the Law, by faith alone. Yes, in spite of all our misdeeds, transgressions and sins, in spite of greatest, most gruesome, most repulsive, heaven-defying, despiteful, most insolent, God-insulting, most satanic misdeeds, transgressions, and sins; we still in spite of all become righteous before God by faith, by faith only and alone. He who by faith lays hold of the Lord Jesus Christ and His righteousness is righteous before God, whoever he or she may be. Of all this which I have just said I take back not one word. Do you hear that? We become righteous before God without the deeds of the Law by faith alone. Where then is boasting? There is none—none at all.

Therefore, if you are concerned about and have to deal with being justified before God—and, that you have to, indeed, in any moment of your life, but especially in the moment of death—then you must without fail cling to this, "apart from works of the law." Then you must look away altogether from yourself and look only to Christ. Look away completely from works and look only to Christ's work done for you, and then speak to your heart by the Holy Spirit and say, "Christ and His work done for me is my righteousness." That is the faith that justifies. Yes, and you dare not depend or count on, you dare not think, that God will in any way count to your credit your deep feeling of sorrow over your sin and this your sorrowful sighing because of your sinful condition. You can ground your faith and hope alone on Christ, Who is set before you as your Righteousness in God's Word. That is the justifying faith. And, therefore we conclude that a man is "justified by faith apart from works of the law" (3:28).

Like that, and in no other way, is a man made righteous in God's sight, whoever he may be, Jew or Gentile, circumcised or not. Or, "is God the God of Jews only? Is he not the God of Gentiles also?" (3:29). Of course, He is the God also of the Gentiles, if indeed God is one (as He surely is) Who will justify by faith the circumcised and the uncircumcised through faith. And, therefore we conclude that a man, whoever he may be, becomes righteous without the deeds of the Law, by faith alone.

That is the justifying faith. But what about the Law? "Do we then overthrow the law by this faith? By no means! On the contrary, we uphold the law" (3:31). We place it before our attention for our good and its proper meaning. But, more of this later. For now let each of us see well to himself that he is righteous before God, which happens without the works of the Law, by faith alone.

Letter XI
Abraham, Justified by Faith in Christ

<u>Romans 4</u>

Therefore, we conclude that a man is justified before God apart from works of the law through the faith in Jesus Christ. Never otherwise, never!

Let's take Abraham, the ancestor of the Old Testament people of God, the Jewish people, who lived almost at the halfway point between Adam and Christ. What of Abraham? What did he find according to the flesh; namely, what did he achieve by his own doing and work? You see, if Abraham was made righteous by works, then he has something to boast of before God. But, we have to say that's not the way it was before God and according to God's judgment. God did not give Abraham the chance to boast at all. "For what does the Scripture say? 'Abraham believed God, and it was counted to him as righteousness'" (4:3). Abraham believed God's Word and promise of Christ, and through this believing (faith) he was made righteous in God's sight out of pure grace. "Now to the one who works, his wages are not counted as a gift but as his due. And to the one who does not work but believes in him who justifies the ungodly, his faith is counted as righteousness" (4:4–5). That is the way it was with Abraham. Abraham believed that God would make the godless and God-despising world righteous through Christ (the Messiah). By that faith he laid hold of the promised righteousness for his own personal self, and became righteous before God and was justified. Exactly so it is now with us Christians also (4:1–5).

We believe that God has made the whole godless world of sinners righteous in Christ, has justified it, and we—like Abraham—draw this justification through faith into our own person and accept it. And so we have it and are through that faith righteous and justified. In this same way, King David, who lived about halfway between Abraham and Christ, declares blessed that man to whom God imputes righteousness; namely, the righteousness of Christ, without works. He says, "Blessed are those whose lawless deeds are forgiven, and whose sins are covered; blessed is the man against whom the Lord will not count his sin" (4:7–8). As we know, forgiveness and covering of unrighteousness and sins and not charging sin to one's account is the same as imputation of righteousness, declaring one righteous, or justification (4:6–8).

Now to proceed. To whom and to what kind of person does this beatification or "calling one blessed" pertain or apply? Does it pertain to the circumcised, to Jews? Or does it also apply to the uncircumcised, the Gentiles? We have said, as you know, that for Abraham his faith was imputed to him for righteousness. How was his faith imputed to him and when? When he was already circumcised, or when he was yet uncircumcised? Not when he was already circumcised, but when he was yet uncircumcised. And he received the sign of circumcision first of all, as a divine seal of the righteousness that comes through the faith—through that faith which he already had when he was yet uncircumcised. And so Abraham was meant to be a spiritual father and a forever valid type and sign for all those who believe as uncircumcised ones, as Gentiles. Also to these the righteousness was to be imputed. And Abraham was meant to be a spiritual father, an ever-valid type, and a sign for the circumcised ones, for the Jews, his descendants; namely, for those who are not only circumcised outwardly, but also follow in the footsteps of the faith of their father Abraham. This faith he had when he was yet uncircumcised—also, to those who follow in the footsteps of faith, the righteousness was to be imputed or credited. In other words, Gentiles and Jews and all people, like Abraham, were to be made righteous before God without the deeds of the Law, by faith alone. And, all believers were so to become the spiritual seed, the spiritual children, of Abraham (4:9–12).

For consider also the following. The promise of eternal salvation was given to Abraham and to his seed, his spiritual descendants. It was promised to Abraham that he with his seed "would be the heir of the world" (4:13), that is the promised new heaven and new earth, namely salvation, should be his inheritance. But most assuredly, this promise was not given through the Law (as though perchance, somehow he by keeping the Law became righteous before God), but because of the righteousness of faith, because he was righteous before God by faith. Surely anyone can see that! "For if it is the adherents of the law," they who hope to gain salvation by keeping the Law, "be the heirs," then faith would have no object or sense "and the promise is void" (4:14). For through the Law comes no salvation, "for the law brings wrath" (4:15). The Law brings only God's anger and displeasure because no man keeps or can keep it. "But where there is no law there is no transgression," (4:15) but the Law is and does exist, and consequently, also transgression—and so does God's wrath and damnation. But the inheritance of salvation comes not through the Law. Therefore, the inheritance must come out of faith, so that it may come in the only way in which it can possibly come; namely, by grace (4:13–16).

"That is why it depends on faith, in order that the promise may rest on grace and be guaranteed to all his offspring" (4:16), for all believers. Not to that seed only which is of the Law, not only to those who descend from Abraham according to the flesh (the believing Jews who had the Law of Moses), "but also to the one who shares the faith of Abraham" (4:16), who are by birth Gentiles, but have the faith that Abraham had, "who is the father of us all" (4:16). And so Abraham is the spiritual father of all believers, their ever-valid prototype (pattern) and ideal, whom they do and must imitate and copy. This God Himself tells us as it is written, "I have made you the father of many nations" (4:17); namely, the father of all believers in many nations, wherever and whenever they might be living on earth. This is the way Abraham stood in God's eyes before God as the spiritual father of all believers. Abraham stood before God Whose Word and promise concerning Christ he believed, and Who awakens the spiritually dead to faith and calls into existence the spiritual children of Abraham who in Abraham's day were not yet here.

Yes, Abraham believed God's Word and the promise of Christ. God produced this faith in him in order to make him the father of many nations as said above. God told him when He showed him the stars of heaven saying, "So shall your offspring be" (Gen.

15:5). For even though at the time there may have been only a few believers on earth, in the end, when all are taken together they equal a vast and unnumbered host indeed.

Abraham believed, believed contrary to all human hope. Nevertheless, on the basis of this God-given hope, he did not weaken in faith nor abandon his trust. When God promised him Isaac and in Isaac, Christ Himself, Abraham, "considered his own body, which was as good as dead (since he was about a hundred years old), or when he considered the barrenness of Sarah's womb. No unbelief made him waver concerning the promise of God, but he grew strong in his faith as he gave glory to God, fully convinced that God was able to do what he had promised" (4:19–22). For by faith Abraham laid hold on Christ and Christ's righteousness.

All this is also written for us, and primarily for us and for our benefit. To us the righteousness of Christ shall be credited and imputed; we shall be justified, we who believe on Him who raised up Jesus our Lord from the dead. For our Lord Jesus "was delivered up for our trespasses" (4:25) into death, to atone for our sins, and "raised for our justification" (4:25), in order that all of us should in Him be declared free of all sin, also of our sin, and be justified before God. So then, let us trust and believe on our Lord Jesus Christ, that we through faith may possess that righteousness procured by Him for all the world (4:23–25).

Letter XII
The Consequences of Justification

Romans 5:1–11

What do we have now that we are righteous before God by faith? Of what benefit is our justification to us?

What questions! If God no longer charges us with any sins, but declares us innocent, just, clean, and holy—that surely must have the most blessed consequences for us. Let me speak to you of this in this letter.

"Therefore, since we have been justified by faith, we have peace with God through our Lord Jesus Christ" (5:1). Now we have peace with God. God is not angry with us anymore. God, before Whom we are by nature such arrogant sinners, miserable, helpless worms, good-for-nothings, no longer has anything against us, neither does He judge or condemn us. We need not tremble in fear of the greatest of all evils; namely, eternal, fiery damnation, which most certainly would have to come upon us if God would still war and fight against us. God is now pleased with us. He has declared the peace, He Himself. "Her warfare is ended" (Is. 40:2). All this God has done through our Lord Jesus Christ. "Through him we have also obtained access by faith into this grace in which we stand, and we rejoice in hope of the glory of God" (5:2). Confidently, with heavenly rapture and ecstasy we lift up our heads and boast ourselves of this our God-given hope, the hope of future glory we will share in endless blessed eternity with our reconciled God! Heaven is ours! We are going to be with Jesus!

But, we boast not only in hope of future glory that God will give us. We also boast with confident rejoicing in suffering which we must still endure. "Knowing that suffering produces endurance" (5:3), for our sufferings are first dipped in love by our God's fatherly hand, and will bring us a rich blessing, namely the blessing of a faith in Christ made all the stronger and more durable through these sufferings and trials. For suffering produces endurance, the endurance of trusting faith. Under the grace and blessing of God, our faith learns to defend itself under attack of suffering and becomes patient, enduring, firm and deep-rooted. "And endurance produces character" (5:4), our faith proves itself dependable by this testing. That faith made patient, firm, and durable accumulates a treasure of spiritual experience and proves itself truly genuine. And this "character produces hope" (5:4). The experienced and proven faith looks to its goal: there is the joy of victory! That is the calm and ever forward-reaching hope. "And hope does not put us to shame" (5:5). Who dies in this divinely grounded hope will not be deceived or ashamed, rather he arrives safely in heaven. So God strengthens the saving faith through suffering. And knowing this, we rejoice even in tribulation:

> My heart from care is free,
> No trouble troubles me.
> Misfortune now is play,
> And night is bright as day.[1]

Yes, everything comes into focus, because God focuses everything in our lives upon our salvation. That we know. We know our hope will not embarrass us.

For God's love, our knowledge of God's love, the great love He has for us, "has been poured into our hearts through the Holy Spirit who has been given to us" (5:5). Of this His love to us God keeps telling us in His Word, and through the Holy Spirit Who is given to us with His Word, God gives us that inner divine conviction of His love toward us in our hearts, by power of which He most assuredly will not permit us to be lost, but will save us. In assuring us of His love to us by the Holy Spirit, He makes us divinely certain of our salvation. His love to us guarantees us our salvation. This I will show you now.

Christ, Who Himself is God over all, died for us, the ungodly, in God's duly appointed time when we were still without strength (5:6). What were we when Christ died for us? We, who are alive

---

[1] Paul Gerhardt, "Awake My Heart, With Gladness," stanza 5.

today, were not even here. But what were we in God's eyes? We were "still weak" (5:6), unfit to stand in His sight, unfit to gain salvation. We were "ungodly" when Christ died for us. That surpasses all human comprehension. Human love "will scarcely die for a righteous person—though perhaps for a good person one would dare even to die" (5:7). But, would anyone give his life for someone who was evil and wicked, a wretched lawbreaker? Certainly not. "But God shows his love for us in that while we were still sinners, Christ died for us" (5:8). When we were unfit, godless sinners, and an abomination in His sight, He gave His life to buy us for Himself. What kind of love is that! If that is true, then you tell me, dear Christian friends: how much more will His love compel Him to save us from wrath to come, since we are now justified through the blood of Jesus (5:9)?

When we were still enemies God loved us so that He reconciled us to Himself through the death of His only-begotten, eternal Son (5:10). But now we have become His reconciled, dearly beloved children who stand and rejoice in His grace, all through the justifying faith He worked in our hearts. "More than that," moved by His Holy Spirit, "we also rejoice" and exult "in God" (5:11), that He is now our dear Father Who has only our best at heart for us for time and eternity. We exult in this on the ground of His unbreakable Word in joyful faith in our Lord Jesus, through Whom we now receive the all-perfect atonement or reconciliation with our God as our eternal possession (5:11). How much more will we then be rescued and saved by God's love! Yes, how much more will we now, since we are now God's friends, share in the life and glory of Him Who gave His life unto death for us when we were still enemies! Indeed, the love of God guarantees us everlasting life.

These are the blessed consequences of justification. But, dear Christians, forever keep your eyes on the sure Word, which gives you this justification, and never on the changeable and deceptive clouds that would darken the light of your joy and confidence. The Word comes from God, the clouds from yourselves. Which will you have?

Letter XIII
Adam and Christ

Romans 5:12–21

We, miserable lost and condemned sinners, become righteous before God and are saved without the deeds of the Law, by faith alone. Jesus Christ has made good all the loss that we inherited from Adam's fall. That is why we wish to place Adam and Christ in contrast to each other now. And, God granting it, we hope to derive genuine joy and blessedness by doing so.

Through one man sin came into the world of men. By the fall of Adam, sin made its entrance on earth. And through sin, came death. Through Adam's sin, death—the wages of sin—made its entrance into this world. Death. What is death? Death is not only that final dying. No, death is the entire condition (or plight) in which we find ourselves because of sin. The germ, the power of death is in us from the first moment of our existence. The child in the womb, the newborn child, has death in itself. Death is rampant in us every way as long as we live. A decaying tooth, a bothersome abscess, proves it. We die, one early the other in later years. Then death continues on and on in eternal ruin and perdition. That's how Adam was in death, *not* from the day he was created, oh no, but from the day he fell into sin. So also Eve. And so, through Adam's fall, "death spread to all men because all sinned" (5:12b). Death was transmitted, perpetuated onward into all of Adam's posterity—by and because of Adam's fall into sin. Why? "Because all sinned" (5:12). What does that mean? Does it mean that all of them really and in truth committed sin?

It is, of course, true that all men have really in very truth committed sin and will continue to do so. But surely the meaning cannot be that death passed from Adam to all men, because each for himself actually committed sin. For if this were the first cause, the fountainhead of this universal, all-infecting death, then this death would not have penetrated on through from Adam to all men. Then, all men would have each contaminated himself with death and each would have drawn it into himself afresh and anew. No, death is passed on from Adam to all mankind. Why? Because they all in Adam have sinned. Adam was, as it were, yes Adam actually was the seed-kernel out of which the whole of mankind grew into being. And now when Adam sinned and became a sinner, all men then sinned in him and became sinners. And as a result, death also penetrated on through to all men. So it is. So God has spoken. So God has established and fixed it fast. This, of course, does not go down very well with us; it is hard for us to swallow. But here nothing will do any good. You may turn and twist, you might rationalize and argue as you will; it won't help, it *is* that way. From Adam "death spread to all men," (5:12) for as said before, in Adam all men have sinned.

One can also see this to some degree. Sin, you see, was in this world from Adam's to Moses' time: that is, until the day when the Law was given through Moses. But it was not until the Law was given, that sin became a direct and clear transgression of the divine Law with those who had it. And then it was clear and obvious that the transgressors deserved death. "But sin is not counted (charged to) where there is no Law" (5:13).

That is a universally accepted rule of conduct and judgment. For where there is no Law, there one cannot say that one has transgressed it, and so cannot punish one for it. But during the years when the Law of Moses was not yet here; namely, from Adam's time to Moses, was death during that time not in the world? Oh, most certainly. "From Adam to Moses death reigned even over them that had not sinned after the similitude of Adam's transgression" (5:14), who knowingly transgressed a clearly and distinctly stated commandment of God—for these as you know did not have such a clearly and distinctly stated commandment of God, because the commandment of God through Moses had not yet been given. You see it then, that death passed through to them because in Adam they all had sinned, as said before. But, perhaps you would want to argue here and say, "The Law of God was written into their hearts, wasn't it? And so they certainly had it." I say, "That is true." They had the Law to some degree or measure, and enough to make them inexcusable; namely, guilty and so under divine wrath. But, how is it with the little children, with the newborn children? What do they know of the Law? And yet so many die. You see, it's as clear as day, death passed upon all mankind because in Adam they all sinned.

And this Adam is now a picture of Him, who was still to come; namely, Christ. It's like this: as sin and death came upon all men through Adam, so the gift of grace, righteousness, and life came upon all men. Anyone sees that.

But, there is a vast difference between the gift of grace that came through Jesus Christ, and the awful consequences of Adam's fall into sin. The gift of grace more than tips the scales against the dire consequences of The Fall. "For if many (people) died through one man's trespass (Adam), much more have the grace of God and the free gift (which comes) by the grace of that one man Jesus Christ abounded for many," is overwhelmingly sufficient for those same many people (5:15). God would much rather give love than punishment. God's passion of love is far greater than that of His wrath. God spared not His Son, God's Son didn't even spare Himself, only to give us the gift of righteousness and life. The tides of grace roar mightier by far than those of wrath.

Yes, the situation is vastly different between the gift of righteousness and life which God gives us, and the frightening consequences of Adam's fall into sin. For from the one who has sinned (Adam), came the judgment of God to condemnation (5:16). But the free gift of God's grace covers not only the one sin of Adam and the sins of all men in Adam. It covers also the many thousands of millions of actual committed sins of the many; many sins of people of all times. Christ justifies them before God and pardons all their sins. And if according to God's judgment, death now reigns through the one (Adam), then much more and sooner by far, they who receive and grasp by faith the great abundance of grace and the ever-so-rich gift of righteousness, shall reign as kings in life everlasting through that One, Jesus Christ (5:16–18).

Oh sinners, you sinful mortals! The ocean of God's grace for righteousness and life overwhelms and covers you mightier than the floods of sin and wrath. Don't you run away in foolish unbelief. Let yourselves gladly be covered by God's grace in faith!

Well then, how is it with Adam and Christ? How are they to be compared? Like this, "Therefore, as one trespass led to condemnation for all men, so one act of righteousness leads to justification and life for all men. For as by the one man's disobedience the many were made sinners, so by the one man's obedience the many will be made righteous" (5:18–19). By Adam's Fall all mankind was damned to death, and by Christ's vicarious (substitutionary) righteousness all mankind is made righteous, and so has eternal life. For, because of the disobedience of the one person the many people were set before God as sinners, and because of the One (Christ) the many people, the very same many people, are set before God as righteous. As in Adam all mankind became condemned sinners, so in Christ all are justified in order that they will inherit eternal life. That's the way it is. It is God's own truth and Word. No one may presume to cut or take anything away from that. And, now everything depends on faith alone, that you now accept that which has been given to you and to all people long ago in Christ. And, what is that? The justification of life. Believe that, you have that; believe that not, you have that not.

Yes, but now how about the Law? Where and how does the Law now fit into this? The Law does not break off one tiny iota from what has been said above. The Law has entered with and beside this of what has been said of Adam and Christ (5:20). It came in beside this, in order that the offence of Adam by which we all became sinners, might abound, might increase and grow yet more and more with us, producing all sorts and many sins and transgressions. Why that? In order that we truly understand and see how sinful and hopelessly damned we really are. "But, where sin increased, grace abounded all the more" (5:20). Where by the Law our sin-debt proved to be beyond all bounds, there our grace-credit proved to be far, far beyond even that! Do you hear this, Christians? So, you see, the Law nips off not one iota from what has been said. That's the way it is, and shall be, "So that, as sin reigned in death, grace also might reign through righteousness leading to eternal life through Jesus Christ our Lord" (5:21). Amen!

Letter XIV
The Sanctification of Justified Christians

Romans 6:1–14

"What shall we say then?" (6:1). Say then to what? To what has been said in the last letter and even before that; namely, that where sin abounded, grace abounded boundlessly more. "Are we to continue in sin" and keep on sinning "that grace may abound" (6:1), that God's love and grace would become ever greater and greater? Our enemies, the opponents of the doctrine of justification without the works of the Law, by faith alone, mock us saying that this is what we mean. "By no means!" (6:2). Perish the very thought! "How can we who died to sin still live in it?" (6:2). We who died to sin, how is it possible, that we should still want to keep on living in sin?

With this firmly in mind we come to the Third Chief Part of the Epistle to the Romans, the one that deals with the sanctification of Christians. By "sanctification" we mean that justified Christians no longer live in sin, no longer serve sin, as though sin were still their master, but rather live to please God and serve Him, through Jesus Christ their Lord.

We justified Christians have died to sin; as a result, we no longer live in sin.

Now, what does this mean? Before a person is justified by faith, sin is his master and ruler. His whole life, actions, thinking, and planning are ruled, directed, and regulated by sin. But after a person has been justified through faith, he has died to sin: meaning that God has made the justified person dead to sin so that it can no longer be his master and boss, can no more control, rule, direct, and regulate his life and doing, his thinking, and aspirations.

But, how is this? How did it come about? And what follows? Listen!

You know, of course, that the gospel is the power of God. The gospel operates in the believer with its power. It unites and ties the believers so tightly and powerfully into one with Christ, that Christ is now their Head and the believers His body and members. In this way, everything that Christ is and has comes to and into the Christian through the gospel. Christ's death with all its power and energy flows to the believers. The death of Christ was the death of reconciliation: by His death the believers have full reconciliation with God. Christ's life with all power and energy flows to the believers. Christ's resurrection to life was His justification, and in Him, the justification of the whole world. Believers have justification to eternal life. Through His death, Christ, however, also was cut free of our sin which He had freely taken on Himself. This our sin, which had become His sin, made His life from beginning to end a life under the power, control, and tyranny of sin. He, by His flawless, immaculate, infinitely holy life, death, and resurrection, victoriously destroyed sin and sin's rule, control, and tyranny. He is free; *we* are free!

Of our sin, Christ freed Himself by His death. They who believe in Him, therefore, were made free of the sin, which until they became believers, was their tyrannical owner and slave driver controlling their entire lives, thinking, and behavior. The believers in Christ have, with Christ, died to sin, become dead to sin. Sin can no more be their master and lord, can no longer control, regulate, and manipulate their life, thinking, planning, and destiny. They are no longer under sin's dominion and control. And Christ's life, His life after His resurrection, is a life totally set free from our sin and from its jurisdiction. Christ now lives unto God alone. His believers, free from sin's power and dominion, live in and with Christ unto God and serve Him here in time and finally into eternity. All this comes through the gospel in faith.

Do you understand this? Meditate upon it diligently! Reflect, ponder, contemplate, and rejoice! You are free!

Now, I wish to speak to you about our baptism. Of baptism, everything is true in every respect of what I have just told you of the gospel, for baptism belongs to the gospel, is part and parcel of it. But, baptism is the divinely ordained, solemn beginning of the state of being a Christian, a believer in Christ, of being a dear child of God. All who were baptized as little children were there and then made believers in Christ. All who became believers in Christ through the gospel as adults, are there in their baptism positively identified and recognized as believers in Christ. And, I now want to speak about us and to you, who have been baptized and believe.

Dear Christians, you now know and understand the following. We all were baptized into Christ and were united through our baptism with Christ. With Christ we died. We were buried with Him in baptism into death. We were set free with Him from the dominion of sin. With Christ we died unto sin. What for? For what purpose? "In order that, just as Christ was raised from the dead by the glory of the Father, we too might walk in newness of life" (6:4), a life released and free from the control and tyranny of sin. "For if we have been united with him (with Christ) in a death like his, we shall certainly be united with him in a resurrection like his" (6:5). For, if we were planted through baptism into Christ and became grown together with Him, so that His death is our death and we so become like Him in death, then we are also planted in Him and grown together with Him, so that His resurrection and life belong to us, and we become like Him in His resurrection and life. Why, of course! Knowing this, that our old man (our old sin-man) is crucified with Him—for what purpose? "That the body of sin," that our sin-body, this instrument and tool of sin and her cravings and desires, "might be brought to nothing," might lose its power and strength, "so that we would no longer be enslaved to sin" (6:6). "For," as you well know, it is a universally accepted principle that, "one who has died has been set free from sin" (6:7). He is no longer under sin's control and power. So we died with Christ and are declared free from sin, rid of sin's control and power. This we firmly believe. But, "now if we have died with Christ, we believe that we will also live with him. We know that Christ, being raised from the dead, will never die again; death no longer has dominion over him. For the death he died he died to sin, once for all, but the life he lives he lives to God" (6:8–10). Therefore, you dear Christians, because through baptism the death and the life of Christ was made yours, and you are grown together with it, "consider yourselves dead to sin," free from the power and control of sin, "and alive to God in Christ Jesus" (6:11).

That is the sanctification (holy-making) of the justified Christian. And, this is the power of the sanctification of the justified Christian, that this sanctification emanates, proceeds, not from ourselves, but from our Lord Jesus Christ, from His death and from His life. Of His death and life we share and partake through baptism in faith, and likewise of all the power of this death and this life. Of course, we who know this, we indeed still commit sin because we still are in this mortal body. Sin, with all its lusts and desires still clings to us as long as we live on earth. But, reign over and control us, that sin shall not do. In faith, we constantly lift ourselves up to Christ, who is given to us as our very own through the means of grace (gospel and sacraments). From Him, we receive grace upon grace, for constant forgiveness and justification, as well as strength for strength again and always again for a new and better life.

Oh, Christians, you baptized, believing Christians. Since you have such grace and strength in Christ, "Let not sin therefore reign in your mortal body" (6:12a). Do not heed its coaxing and enticing desires, "To make you obey its passions. Do not present your members to sin as instruments for unrighteousness, but present yourselves to God as those who have been brought from death to life, and your members to God as instruments for righteousness" (6:12b–13). For sin will have no dominion over you (any longer), since you are not under law" (6:14), which can indeed demand and demand, but gives you no power to do it. No, but you are "under grace," grace that gives you strength to reject and avoid the evil and to do the good. This is the sanctification of the justified Christian.

Letter XV
Justified Christians Are Happy Servants of Righteousness

Romans 6:15–23

 Well, then, what follows? In the previous letter it was demonstrated that we justified Christians no longer live under the sternly demanding Law but under friendly, ever-giving grace. So then, what now? Go right on and sin all we please because we are not under the Law but under grace? Never, my Christian friends! "By no means! Do you not know that if you present yourselves to anyone as obedient slaves, you are slaves of the one whom you obey," whether you give yourselves willingly as a servant to sin, then you are on the way to death, but if you give yourselves as servants to obedience of righteousness, then you finally arrive to the point where righteousness, the doing of the right, becomes second nature, or a happy necessity to you (6:15–16).

 Oh, happy Christians, thank God that you, who once were servants to sin and who were, perhaps, at one time even miserable slaves to sin—thank God, it's different now! Now, you have become a true believer at heart. God made you a sincere heart-believer. God has worked in you the obedience of faith. God has bound your heart, spirit, and disposition to His Word of grace, which is the true original and ideal and form, the only guide-rule of free and saving doctrine. Into this bondage, or imprisonment God has given or placed you. Thus, you were set free from the bondage and imprisonment of sin, and have been made servants—willing, happy servants—of righteousness to holiness. You now don't want to serve sin. In fact, you cannot commit sin. You now must, in response to that inner, ardent, yet blessed urgency, be servants of righteousness. You really cannot do otherwise; you don't want it otherwise. You find yourselves compelled to live unto holiness.

And whenever sin does overpower you, you take refuge to God's grace, and in grace you quickly return at once to righteousness unto holiness. It's truly a blessed, happy servitude to righteousness (6:17–18).

To speak of "servitude or slavery to righteousness," to say that justified Christians have become "slaves of righteousness," is obviously a form of speech which is found nowhere else in Holy Scripture. Scripture does speak of servitude of sin and of servants or slaves of sin, but not of servitude and slaves of righteousness. This is "speaking in human terms" (6:19) which accommodates itself very clearly, perhaps even crassly to our human concepts and imagination. Yet, it is good to speak of this subject in this manner, because of the infirmity or limitations which originate in our flesh, our troublesome, encumbering flesh and blood. We do not really understand, we just cannot visualize it as powerfully as we must, that we justified Christians have nothing whatsoever to do with sin, but are ruled altogether by righteousness, living totally unto holiness. But, this we are truly and actually to do. This is now our new existence, our new state of being. We are now new persons. And, if we really consider and weigh it rightly by the power of the Holy Spirit in faith, we really want to have it like that. We are, we should be, and want to be free of sin. We are, should be, and truly want to be servants of righteousness.

Therefore, dear Christians, let me tell you this! Even as you, when you were yet unbelievers, have yielded your members as servants to uncleanness and to iniquity unto iniquity; even so now yield your members as serviceable instruments of righteousness unto holiness. For when you were servants of sin you were free as far as righteousness was concerned (6:20). But, what sort of freedom was that? A miserable freedom, indeed! Righteousness for you was out of the question; you couldn't produce it, you didn't want to produce it. You were totally cut off and free of it. You were even glad that you were! Well, what did you at that time bring forth? "But what fruit were you getting at that time from the things of which you are now ashamed?" (6:21a). Those fruits were disgraceful, heinous vices and unrighteousness, "for the end of those things is death" (6:21b) and finally leads to eternal death.

"But now that you have been set free from sin and have become slaves of God" by faith in Jesus Christ, "the fruit you get leads to sanctification and its end, eternal life," a different fruit, indeed (6:22). You occupy yourselves in a holy and godly way of life before God and mankind. You exert yourselves to prove your love and gratitude to God with good works and to help your neighbor in love in both body and soul. And even though such sanctified life is, indeed, quite imperfect because of sin that still clings to you, God is nevertheless delighted and well-pleased with it, because you are His beloved, and by grace, adopted children. And you, too, are glad and joyful as such. The end of this is everlasting life! The blessed end of the way of sanctification!

Mark it well, dear Christians, and do understand this rightly, "For the wages of sin is death" (6:23a). He who gives himself to sin, serves sin, is an obedient servant of sin, will receive his due, his wages: death! And don't forget what death is. Not only the dying, but also that into which death takes you: eternal death, everlasting damnation. This death will be the well-deserved and unfailing lot of the servant of sin. This death, which came upon all men already through Adam's sin and in whom all of us sinned—this death remains upon the servant of sin. In his black lap, this death has more than enough riches of frightful horrors to pay the service of sin promptly and well. On the other hand, however, "the free gift of God is eternal life in Christ Jesus our Lord" (6:23). That gift no human being can earn, acquire, or get by himself, not with the most faithful and consistent holiness, nor with the most diligent service of righteousness. That is a pure gift of God's grace, purchased and won for us by Jesus Christ, and presented to us in Christ Jesus, with Christ Jesus. Alone by the faith, without the works of the Law will it ever be gained by us and become our own. These who are justified without the deeds of the Law by faith alone are therewith also at the same time heirs of eternal life. And, mark it well, you Christians! On this way of sanctification, on the way of servitude to righteousness, God leads the justified ones onward toward and into this their goal, the happy ending of their earthly existence, everlasting life. There is no other way. The justified Christians are, you see, set free from sin's slavery and have entered upon a new life in God, the life in God which had its beginning through the new God-life of Christ when He was raised to life from death again.

Liberated from sin's tyranny, happy servants of God, they travel onward to their heavenly goal, everlasting life. What a blessed highway, what a happy goal! Happy servants of righteousness, how gladly they let themselves be guided by God on the Highway of Holiness that leads into everlasting life!

Isn't this the way you feel about it, dear Christian friends? That's the way it is with every justified Christian.

However, therein lies a warning; a strong, strident warning for us all. We dare not fall away from the faith. We dare not let ourselves be charmed and cheated by the beguiling eyes of sin, and so enter her service again. That ends in death! We must remain in the faith. We must remain servants of righteousness. Then, and only then, will we enter into eternal life. God, our reconciled heavenly Father for the sake of our Lord Jesus Christ, help us by His Holy Spirit! And, He will! Amen.

Letter XVI
The Christian's Happy Freedom from the Law

Romans 7:1–6

There is more, a good deal more, about sanctification. Until now, we have learned that we justified Christians have been liberated from the slavery of sin and become servants of righteousness unto holiness, because in and with Christ we died to sin and entered upon a new life centered upon God. It was also briefly noted that sin for that reason will not have dominion over us, because now we are no longer under the Law, but under grace. And precisely this thought, this sacred truth of Holy Writ, will now be set forth in detail and offered for your understanding of faith.

"Or do you not know, brothers—for I am speaking to those who know the law—that the law is binding on a person only as long as he lives?" (7:1). As long as a person lives, the Law gives him commandments and demands obedience from him. But no longer. Beyond this life, the Law cannot go. After death, to be sure, the transgressor receives his punishment as threatened by the Law, but the demanding and commanding of the Law, the entire Law, in fact, exists no longer for man. The jurisdiction of the Law is only for this earthly life. Consider as an example the sixth commandment concerning the conjugal relationship between husband and wife. By this commandment the espoused wife is bound to the husband as long as he lives. But when the husband has died, the wife has been set free from the law concerning the man. As long as the husband is alive, the woman is rightly called an adulteress if she yields herself to someone else. "But if her husband dies, she is free from the law of marriage" (7:2b) which bound her to the man. "But if her husband dies, she is free from that law, and if she marries another man she is not an adulteress" (7:3). The law concerning spouses is no longer in effect if one of the spouses has died. The surviving wife has, by his death, died to the law concerning the departed man. She is dead to the law which formerly bound her. She is free!

In the same, identical manner, you, my brothers, were also made dead to the Law; yes, to the entire Law with all its commandments, by the body of Christ. What does this mean that "you also have died to the law through the body of Christ" (7:4a)? This, in fact: in your place and stead, Christ, as your Substitute, had been placed under the Law. There He firstly kept and fulfilled all demands of the Law, and secondly, bore all the curse of the Law. And then when He died physically in His body, He delivered to the Law the most perfect and most exhaustive satisfaction in every possible detail regarding its demands as well as its threats and curses. There Christ was finished with the Law, completely finished! The Law was not even there for Him anymore. In no respect did He have anything more to do with it. He had died to the Law, was made dead to the Law. All this He did in our stead for us as our Substitute. Oh, I wanted to say, "For you, in your place, as your Substitute! And now through the gospel, by faith, you have partaken of Christ, have been in-grown, grown together with Him. You have partaken of His death, grown together with His death, through which He died to the Law, was killed to the Law." So then, dear Christians, in this way you have become dead to the Law by the body of Christ. You are now finished, totally finished with the Law. The Law is not there for you anymore ever; whether it be for its threats, its curses, or its demands. Now you have nothing to do anymore with the Law in any way whatever. You have died to the Law. You have been made dead to the Law (7:4).

Do you get it? Does it penetrate? Savvy? Who is it here shaking his head? I say it again, and most emphatically, "You now have absolutely nothing more to do with the Law, with that Holy Law of God—in no way, in no respect whatever! The Law—its threats, demands, commands—is none of your business anymore. It's not there for you. It's out of existence for you. You are dead to the Law. It can't touch you ever again. It's been made dead by the body of Christ." Only believe that, dear Christians. God tells you that! It is God's teaching. Take it deadly seriously! Woe to you, if even one solitary curse or one solitary demand of the Law would still apply to you or concern you! But the Law is of no concern to you at all, anymore.

Listen you dear Christians, especially you who have been shaking your heads, you have become dead to the Law by the body of Christ, that you should be married to another, even to Him who is raised from the dead, Jesus Christ our Lord (7:4).

Mark it well, we justified Christians did not only become partakers of Christ's death through the gospel by faith, not only grown together with His death as we have just demonstrated it; no, we also became partakers of His life. We were also grown together with His God-life. Liberated, set free by His death from the dominion of the Law, we are now bound into one, united in the most intimate manner with the Risen One, the Ever-Living One. We are spiritually married to our living Lord. What is His is ours. But our love and faithfulness and obedience in all things belong to Him. To Him alone. To no one else. His Word alone counts for us; He alone tells us what to do, and in doing that, in telling and directing us, He gives us the abilities of His life that we hear and obey. No, we are under no other but Him. We are no longer under the Law. As far as concerns the Law, we are made dead to it by His body. But we live unto our Lord, we are His, we hear His voice, we follow Him. How blessed we are, belonging to Christ! He clothes us in His righteousness, He daily and richly forgives us all our sins. He also gives us His Holy Spirit and the strength of His new God-life. He leads, guides, and teaches us to walk with more than a mother's love and patience on the new path of holiness to eternal life. He does that in order that we should bring forth fruit unto God, our Father and His Father. This fruit is the fruit of a holy way of life and good works; namely, the fruit which we were not able to produce before when we were not yet His, that is, when we were still under the Law.

For consider as well, dear Christians, how the matter really stands. As long as we do not yet belong to Christ, as long as we have not yet by faith become His own, so long as we are still in the flesh, in our own corrupt nature, we remain under the Law which then rules over us with its commands and prohibitions. But what happens in such a case? Our flesh cannot obey the Law, and it doesn't even want to. What says the hymn?

> Our flesh has not those pure desires
> The spirit of the Law requires,
> And lost was our condition.[2]

On the contrary, precisely through the Law and its commandings and forbiddings, the lusts and violent passions of all sorts of sins are awakened in us and raised to action. These lusts and sinful passions then use the members of our bodies to satisfy themselves in all sorts of vices and lawlessness. And so these lusts and sinful passions become powerful and active in the members of our bodies to bring forth fruit, fruit of sin—unto death, of course, everlasting death. "For the wages of sin is death" (6:23). Yes, that's the way it is. Don't you know this? Can't you see how it is? Think it over a bit! In the next letter I shall have more to say of this matter. So it is, as long as we do not belong to Christ, but are in the flesh, we are under the Law (7:5).

But now we have been freed from the Law, from all its control, commanding, and forbidding. We are loosed from this unbearable sin-provoking agent, for you see we have died to our flesh, in which we were by nature held as in prison, and in which we gnashed our teeth against the Law. Our flesh, our corrupt nature, our Old Man has been crucified with Christ. Our body of sin, this instrument and tool of lusts and evil passions aroused by the Law, has ceased holding us imprisoned. And now by faith we belong to our Lord Jesus Christ, so that we now serve God according to the new existence of the living Holy Spirit, not in the old existence of the killing letter of the Law (7:6). Christ our Lord rules us now by His Holy Spirit, so that we now render Him willing obedience. However, we are free from the rule and the control of the Law.

That is the justified Christian's blessed freedom from the Law. Should I, need I, say more to clarify this matter? But this letter is getting too long!

Real short and sweet then.

First, you dear Christians have died, died in Christ to your flesh as well as to the Law. But that does not mean that your flesh and the Law are dead. Your flesh still clings to you, and the Law stands threateningly at the door, at your door. If you fall away from

---

[2] Paul Speratus, "Salvation unto Us Has Come," stanza 2.

Christ, if you fall back into the flesh and into the life of the flesh, you at the same time also fall back under the rule and control of the Law and are then lost. And, it is good that we are reminded of this just because our flesh still clings to us and would pull us away from Christ.

Secondly, you Christians belong to Christ. He alone is your Lord and Master. And through His Holy Spirit He teaches you and writes into your heart a willingness to serve Him, not only that, but also how you should serve Him and bring forth fruit. But your flesh still clings to you. In the first place, your flesh wants to make you unwilling to serve Christ. For that reason it is good, good because of your flesh, that the Law stands at the door and shows the "whip of the driver" now and then and says, as it were, "You must serve God, or else!" Furthermore, your flesh tries to drown out the voice of the Spirit of Christ in you, which tells you how you should serve God and what kind of works please Him. Because of this influence of the flesh, you might want to serve Christ in a manner which is not as the Holy Spirit would have it. And so it is good—because of your flesh—that you look into the Law to learn which are the works that please God. For, as you know, the will of Christ agrees perfectly with the requirements of the Law.

Thirdly, you Christians are not ever under the dominion and rule of the Law, but only and alone under Christ. That means—and mark it well—you serve Christ, never and in no way whatsoever because the Law drives you to it, but because Christ through His Spirit inwardly moves and teaches you to do so with powerful glad impulses of love and gratitude. You justified Christians are indeed happily free of the dominion of the Law.

Letter XVII
The Law and Sin

Romans 7:7–13

So far I have written three letters concerning the sanctification of Christians. It may have seemed to one or the other of you as though our liberation from sin and our liberation from the Law had been placed side by side as equivalents, as equally blessed and happy. For that reason, it is no doubt well, that now, before speaking further concerning sanctification, it be demonstrated in a special letter how the Law and sin relate to one another, or get along with each other.

If it were equally blessed to be set free from the Law as to be set free from sin, what shall we then conclude from this? Is the Law sin? Is it something evil, bad? God forbid! That thought should not even enter our minds. Isn't the Law God's Law?

Yet the Law has very much to do with sin; yes indeed, in three different ways that I shall now demonstrate. And in doing so, I shall—following the Apostle Paul's example—speak of myself, and explain how the Law and sin get along with each other in myself. Even so, of course, it is also with you.

So then, in three diverse ways the Law relates with sin.

First, "If it had not been for the law, I would not have known sin" (7:7). There were in my life (as also in the life of every person) times, circumstances, and conditions in which I lived on and on without the Law. What I mean to say is this: I possessed, of course, the natural knowledge of God's will and the Law of God which is common to all human beings. I had memorized the Ten Commandments very well. But all this was only dead knowledge to me. I didn't think of God's Law, much less did I consider or take it to heart. The Law was lying unused and for that reason, inactive in me, like a locked up Bible on the library table. So I lived on without the Law.

By nature, I was also sinful at that time, of course. But that did not bother me in the least. I committed sins of all sorts every day and in every way, but as long as these did not bring me punishment or pain, I gave it no thought whatsoever. And if they did bring me punishment or pain, then I gave more thought (or concern) to the punishment and pain than to the sins. You see, I just did not understand sin to be what it truly is: a grievous transgression against God's will and Law. And now I considered even those evil thoughts, lusts, and desires as merely natural emotions and impulses—if I gave them any thought at all. All this was so because I lived without the Law. For how can one recognize and be concerned about sin where there is no Law?

But when the Law came, that means, when by God's grace—yes, by His grace—when the Law awoke and came to life in me, when I thought of the well-learned Law, considered it and took it to heart, when I began to realize that the living God stood before me and in His Law said to me, "So you should be! This you should do! That you should not do! You shall not covet!" Then, indeed I recognized sin, also the evil lust, for what it truly is: a constant grievous transgression against God, a constant transgression of God's Law, and an endless being and doing contrary and against God.

In short, I did not know sin except by the Law. Through the Law comes recognition of sin. In this first way, the Law has very much to do with sin.

Second, sin—provoked by the commandment—really did work in me evil lusts of every possible sort.

Yes then, when I, through the Law, saw what sin really was, what then? Did I become a better person? Did I come nearer to God? Start to serve Him from the heart? Did I then sin less and less? The exact opposite happened.

> I sank but deeper into sin.
> There was no good in me at all.
> I was by sin possessed.[3]

---

[3] Martin Luther, "Dear Christians, One and All, Rejoice," stanza 2.

"But sin, seizing an opportunity through the commandment, produced in me all kinds of covetousness" (7:8).

For how is it then really? Without the Law, sin is dead. That simply means that as long as the Law is dead in a person, sin is also dead in him. So long as the Law is dead and does not actively assert itself in his consciousness, so long also is sin dead in a person and is not alive and active in his consciousness. One sins, shall we say, sort of stupidly on and on. A person sins foolishly on and on without really wanting to set oneself against God's will, of Whom he may not even be thinking at all. Without as much as saying, "Now I'm going to sin, transgress God's Law, and insult God." Without thinking, one sins as opportunity presents itself. One may now and then show some common ordinary and commendable natural traits and characteristics. One may even in this way mean to serve God. I also once lived like that without the Law. Even so, the Law and sin were dead in me. But when, as said before, the Law came, when God confronted me with His commandments (especially with, "You shall not covet!"), then sin came to life and leaped into action in me. Prodded into action by the commandment, sin really did work in my naturally corrupt mind and will all kinds of evil desires.

Yes, that is the nature of sin, that's the way it is with our corrupt nature and self. That is fully and completely the way it is with us as long as we are still held captive in sin, in the flesh. The more God's Law wants to suppress sin, so much the more sin rebels against it. The more God's Law forbids evil, the more we want to do it. The more God's Law commands us to do the good, the less we want to do it. As soon as God's Law commands or forbids anything at all, sin—or the flesh in us—is thereby provoked to want the very opposite. In every one of the Ten Commandments; yes, with every more complete explanation and clarification of the Decalog, our sin is prodded into producing the corresponding evil and contrary lust in us. And the mightier and clearer God confronts us with His commandments, the mightier our evil lust rebels against Him. It becomes so much clearer, even to ourselves, that we are fighting and rebelling against God the Almighty. With ever clearer intent and fuller awareness, we begin to hate God and His Law and to wish there were no God at all.

Because of this provocation of the holy Law of God, we sinners become open and deliberate rebels against the Most High God. With gnashing teeth we say, "Must everything, everything be evil, unclean, unrighteous, even the innermost lusts and desires?" So it is! Yes, that's the nature of sin and of our corrupt self. That's the way it is with us precisely and completely, so long as we are imprisoned by sin and our corrupt flesh.

And so it was also with me. Sin took occasion by the commandment, was provoked by the commandment and really worked in me all sorts of evil lusts. In this second manner the Law has indeed very much to do with sin.

Third, the Law caused my death. It killed me. I died, yes, died. With teeth gnashing and despairing, I saw that I was hopeless and helpless against God. I experienced the terrors of death, judgment, and damnation. Now I saw it clearly. This is the end of it all for me! And it turned out that the very Law which was meant to be life to me, brought me death. The Law which one should keep and so have eternal life (which threatens death only to the transgressor), that brought me death. But that was not the fault of the Law; it was the fault of my sin. For my sin, my corrupt nature, my flesh, by using the commandment, deceived me and by it killed me. The commandment as you see, is holy, right, and good. Well then, has that which is holy, right, and good become death to me? Of course not! But rather my sin became my death in that I transgressed the Law (7:9–13). And with all this God, Who turns everything to serve His purpose, had a two-fold purpose. First, my sinful ego and nature should show itself for what it really is: sinful. I was to see clearly how startlingly corrupt I am, in that I even misused the good Law to bring death upon myself. Second, God intended that my sinful ego and nature was to really expose itself for what it really is, sinful beyond imagination, by working its fury out against the Law and its commandments. To repeat, all this occurred in order that I might by all means know myself, my nature and ego, in all its frightful reality. For this, I want to add here (even though it perhaps doesn't belong here), is the only way God leads a person to justifying and saving faith.

So then, the Law became death to me. In this third respect, the Law has very much to do with sin, indeed.

And now, dear Christians, do you see how the deliverance from sin and the deliverance from the Law were compared to one another as equally blessed and good? Delivered from the evil mastery of sin, which set us against God and His Law, we are now also set free from the mastery and slavery of the Law, which can only serve to drive us sinners deeper into sin and death.

LETTER XVIII
THE CONSTANT WARFARE BETWEEN SPIRIT AND FLESH IN THE JUSTIFIED CHRISTIAN

Romans 7:14–25

In the closing of the last letter we stated, "Delivered from the evil mastery of sin, which set us against God and His Law, we are now also set free from the mastery and slavery of the Law, which can only serve to drive us sinners deeper into sin and death."

This, however, should not be understood to mean that we Christians already in this life could be purely "spirit," completely renewed and altogether in harmony with the Spirit of God, as some religious fanatics maintain. No, our "flesh," our old corrupt nature, the sin, still clings to us, and very stubbornly at that, and makes us sinful. However, that previous statement dare also not be understood to mean that we should now discard the Law altogether, and not use it at all, like still other fanatic spirits want to do.

Not so! We know all too well that our knowledge of the will of our Lord, which the Holy Spirit has worked in us and which guides us inwardly is always being dulled and obscured by the flesh. Now because we know that this will of Christ corresponds and agrees exactly with the demands of the Law, we therefore gladly use the Law always to regain a clear knowledge of our Lord's will, since it is the anxious desire of every Christian to be able to fulfill the will of our Lord Jesus Christ.

And so there is this constant struggle in us justified Christians between spirit and flesh: the spirit wants to be obedient to the Law, the flesh does not. Of this I wish to speak now. And again I will do as Paul did, describe my own experiences in doing so. For the experiences of every individual born-again Christian are one and the same.

"For we know that the law is spiritual" (7:14). That is, it conforms and agrees with the Holy Spirit because it is the Law of God. And so we know also that the Law demands a purely spiritual heart and mind and a life and behavior fully in agreement with the Holy Spirit. But how is it with me? How do I find it to be with me every day? I am fleshly, by nature flesh, sinful, yes, sold under sin. Even though I am a Christian, born again, even though I am spiritual and ruled by the Spirit of God, even though I desire to be my Lord's very own, obey Him, and do His will as stated in the Law, despite it all, I find that the flesh clings to me, and that its evil contrary-to-the-Law impulses reach into my innermost heart and mind, and defile all my actions and behavior. I cannot, cannot escape from it! I am simply sold under sin.

> The Law delights my heart, it's true
> And makes me truly glad.
> And yet my flesh so prone to sin
> Mocks me and makes me sad.
> So often I can't help myself
> Trapped by my sinful lusts.
> I cry, caught in the chains of sin,
> "Oh, God, help me, I'm lost!"[4]

For what I actually do accomplish and produce, that I know, recognize, and perceive as not being in agreement with my inner true self, as really coming from me, as agreeable to the real me. For it is not what I would rather do, that I actually do; but, what I hate and detest, that I do. If then I do that which I would not, then it is clear, that in my innermost new, Spirit-produced truthfulness, I agree fully that it is not good. Then it is also clear, that it is no more I that do it (the evil, I mean), but sin that dwells in me. (7:15-17)

I can speak like this and so I do, because I am a born-again person, a Christian. A person who is not born again knows nothing of such a struggle between spirit and flesh, for he is being

---

[4] Simon Dach, "Wenn Gott von allem Bösen," stanza 4.

controlled alone by flesh and in no respect whatever by spirit. His entire self is by sin possessed.

But so I also must speak. Such a struggle between spirit and flesh is the case with me. "For I know that nothing good dwells in me, that is, in my flesh. For I have the desire to do what is right, but not the ability to carry it out" (7:18). I see that to want to do the good, that's easy for me, but the doing of it, the doing it in the manner that is pleasing to my Lord and agreeable to the Law of my Lord, and as I also would only so gladly have it, that ability I do not have. "For I do not do the good I want, but the evil I do not want is what I keep on doing" (7:19). If then I do that which I would not, but do that which I detest with all my heart, then surely it is just as I have said: so it is really no more I that do the evil, but sin that dwells in me (7:20). No, I, my real, most inward self, belongs to the Lord Jesus and wants to serve Him. Yes, that's exactly the way it is. Even though sin grows rampantly into my innermost heart, even though sin may swagger about in my ego, even if sin does pollute my thoughts and will, even though it makes me do evil, it still is not the true me, my real and true heart, my very own intention and will, my very own doing. I, with heart, mind, will, and all my doing belong to the Lord Jesus. And yet, I am accountable for that which sin brings about and does. That is why I flee constantly by faith into the Word of grace for renewed justification and also sanctification. And sin, which so permeates and enslaves me, that is to me nothing more than a repulsive pest and poison which can no longer destroy me, yes, can no more overpower me and enslave me in the full sense of the word. What a battle!

"So I find it to be a law," a rule, this inescapable power determining and controlling me which holds true for my life on earth: I, who want to do the good, always have the evil clinging to me (7:21). "For I delight in the law of God" and rejoice in Him "in my inner being" (7:22), the new man, after my real, true self which is born of God. "But I see in my members another law waging war against the law of my mind and making me captive to the law of sin that dwells in my members" (7:23). In my inner person, in my divinely renewed spirit, there rules the Law of God, the will of my Lord Jesus, making me glad and cheerful. But in the members of my body which are always so ready to do evil, I see that there is a different law in me: the law, the will, the longing, the drive of sin. And this law of sin is forever opposing the law of my spirit, my inner person, taking me captive, chains and binds me, and enslaving me under itself and forces the members of my body into its service.

"Wretched man that I am!" (7:24). Yes, I must confess it, dear God. For, of all the wretchedness of this earthly life, this being sold under sin, this imprisonment under the law of sin, is by far the worst. For I am yours, Lord Jesus, and want to be yours, body and soul. I cry to you, Lord Jesus, "Who will deliver me from this body of death" (7:24) in which I am being plagued like this by sin? You will do it, Lord Jesus Christ! You are going to do it when you, at the time of my death will come and when I am facing the terrors of death, you will speak to my frightened soul, "Take heart, it is I; fear not!" Oh, Lord Jesus, how I long for you and your salvation! But also now already, "Thanks be to God through Jesus Christ our Lord!" (7:25). For my God has surely already done great things for me. He has already set me free, has already set me free from the control of sin and the Law. "So then, I myself serve the law of God with my mind," (7:25) the will of my dear Lord; and only with my flesh; alas, I serve the law of sin.

That, my friends, is the constant struggle between spirit and flesh in the justified Christian. And thanks be to God through Jesus Christ, our Lord, the spirit always wins and comes out on top!

And so:

> Rise, man of God, rise up to fight
> Arise, arise to conquer!
> As long as you are in this world
> There'll be no time to linger.
> He who runs from this bitter strife
> Will not receive the crown of life.
> Up, struggle, fight and conquer![5]

---

[5] Angelus Silesius (Johann Scheffler), "Auf Christenmensch, auf, auf, zum Streit," stanza 1.

Letter XIX
The Justified Christian's Life in the Spirit

Romans 8:1–17

Even though we are Christians justified by faith and most intimately united with our Lord and Savior, sin clings to us, nevertheless, in a very frightful manner. It mauls and tears us inwardly and outwardly. And yet we are, in truth, not under sin's lordship. For, as said in the closing of the last letter, with our liberated mind and spirit we serve the Law of God, the will of our dear Lord, and only with our pest-ridden flesh do we serve the law of sin.

Therefore, there is no condemnation judgment for us who are in Christ Jesus, who walk not after the flesh, but after the Spirit (8:1). There is no condemning judgment for us, I say. The sins we commit, of course are condemnable, but God does not condemn us on their account. God, Who has justified us in Christ, now most graciously closes His eyes to our sins, weaknesses, and failings, and does not even take notice of them. He sees only that in us which comes from the Spirit-produced repentance and so is pleasing to Him. He sees only that we are genuinely serving Him and that we truly hate and detest sin. And according to that He forms His opinion and judges us.

And that is, of course, actually our new life. For as we have already seen, the Holy Spirit is ruling us now through a most wonderful and most gracious law or inner guiding principle, through the law of the life in Christ. That means the Holy Spirit has made us partakers of the resurrection and life of our Lord Jesus Christ through the gospel by faith. He has planted us into the resurrection and life of Christ so that we are now grown into them in such a way that their powers and virtues flow into us, making us able to serve God in true holiness. Remember friends, how it was said before in Letter XIV? That is: the law of the life in Christ Jesus with which the Holy Spirit now governs us, this law of the Spirit has set us free from the law of sin and of death. We are now free so that the law of the Spirit now has the upper hand in us and actually governs us.

For the Law of the Ten Commandments could never have accomplished that, it was just impossible for the Law to do it, because as we have clearly seen, it was "weakened by the flesh" (8:3). Our flesh made it impossible for the Law to bring that about in us. But God did accomplish that in us. Because sin has so corrupted and ruined us, God, in order to redeem and set us free, sent His eternal only-begotten Son to us. And, of course to be sure, God sent Him in the same human flesh and form as our poor sinful flesh, yet without sin. Christ, Who was without sin, took into Himself, as you know, all the weaknesses and shortcomings of our nature brought on by our sin. And so Christ accomplished everything that was necessary for our redemption and liberation from sin. In this way, "by sending his own Son in the likeness of sinful flesh and for sin, he condemned sin in the flesh" (8:3). God condemned and damned sin, which lived in and ruled in our flesh, our ruined nature. Why? In order that sin should lose its power and strength to further control us. And this God did with this purpose in mind, "That the righteous requirement" demanded by the Law "might be fulfilled in us" (8:4). God also did this in order that we now would be able to serve God, do God's will, fulfill God's Law, here in time and there in eternity. Here in time we are in the constant combat and struggle between spirit and flesh. There eternally we will be in ultimate, full heavenly perfection. And this purpose which God had in mind, He really has brought about with us "who walk not according to the flesh but according to the Spirit" (8:4).

But consider, dear Christians, yes consider most diligently, what a razor sharp contrast there is between flesh and spirit, between our "old man" and our "new man." By all means, do not drop back into the slavery of the flesh, but remain firm in the life of the Spirit!

"For those who live according to the flesh," follow and are controlled by the flesh, and "set their minds on the things of the flesh," (8:5a) and obey the flesh. Their thoughts and aims in life are set only on sinful, fleshly things. "But those who live according to the Spirit set their minds on the things of the Spirit" (8:5b). They who follow after the Spirit are obeying the Spirit, have their thoughts and goals in life on the spiritual, God-pleasing things. "For to set the mind on the flesh is death, but to set the mind on the Spirit is life and peace" (8:6). "Spiritual mindedness" is the travel garb (pilgrim garment) of those whom God leads to the peace of everlasting life by His love and grace.

Yes, the entire mind-set of the flesh is death. For what, in truth and actual essence, is the mind-set of the flesh? "Hostile to God" (8:7). For we have seen, haven't we, that the flesh "does not submit to God's law; indeed, it cannot" (8:7). In fact, it rebels and rages against the Law and will of God with every fiber of its being. It really cannot do otherwise. That is its essential and real nature. "Those who are in the flesh," with the mind-set of the flesh, caught and held by the flesh, "cannot please God" (8:8). Try as they may, even their seemingly good and best deeds cannot please God, but are abominations to Him. For remember, God's eyes see in these things always that mind-set, that basic essence of enmity against Him. Nor can these "who are in the flesh" turn themselves away from sin even with the infinitely, slightest modicum. Their total mind-set is nothing but enmity against God. Even if the gospel and the Holy Spirit in the gospel approaches them and wants to convert them, they cannot out of themselves do anything at all but resist and rebel because their mind-set and being is essentially "hostile to God" (8:7). He who is converted is converted alone and altogether by God. God, then, creates in this mind-set of enmity a life-beginning, a newness called 'faith.' And in that instant when even that very first spark of such new life is created, in that instant, when even the slightest longing for the salvation of God offered in the gospel arises, in that very instant that person is converted and born again. For his own carnal, fleshly mind-set is nothing but enmity against God, enmity that flees from, fights against, and pushes back against God. Only and alone in those converted and born-again can this longing for the salvation of God possibly exist.

"You, however, are not in the flesh but in the Spirit, if in fact the Spirit of God dwells in you" (8:9a). Not everyone has the Holy Spirit, and not all are really converted and believing Christians who call themselves Christians and pretend to be Christians.

"Anyone who does not have the Spirit of Christ," Who proceeds from the Father as from the Son also and Who leads to the Son, "does not belong to him" (8:9), but is still in the dark realm of sin and death. "But if Christ is in you" in you by faith, "although the body is dead," mortal, "because of sin," in which the Lord once found you, "the Spirit," your inner nature "is life" everlasting life "because of righteousness" which is of Christ and was given to you and grasped by you in faith (8:10). "If the Spirit of him who raised Jesus from the dead dwells in you, he who raised Christ Jesus from the dead will also give life to your mortal bodies through his Spirit who dwells in you" (8:11). The Holy Spirit given to you is the heavenly pledge and security of your resurrection from death to everlasting life.

And now, brothers, if that is the way it is between "flesh" and "spirit," to which of them are you then indebted? To Whom then do you justly and fairly owe thanks, service, and obedience? "Not to the flesh, to live according to the flesh" (8:12), to be sure. For this you must know, "if you live according to the flesh you will die" (8:13) and be eternally lost. Therefore, by all means, do not think that you may willfully or carelessly give in to the flesh; that it is not so bad since God forgives you your sins and does not look at the weaknesses of your flesh anymore. God forbid! That would be a falling from grace and a falling again under the Law. "but if by the Spirit you put to death the deeds of the body, you will live" (8:13). "For" dear brothers, "all who" and only as many "are led by the Spirit of God are the sons of God" (8:14). Only they are accepted as children of God by grace, who are led by the Holy Spirit to serve God. For the Holy Spirit, Who by faith makes us God's children, He is never inactive and idle within us, but urges us onward to good works in every way. Dear Christians, by all means consider this thoroughly. You are children of God, aren't you? You are just that because the Holy Spirit is leading you. This Holy Spirit Who leads you and Whom "you have received," is not a "spirit of slavery," Who makes you tremble in despairing fear again as you once did when you were still captives of the flesh under tyranny of the Law. "You have received the Sprit of adoption as sons," (8:15) through Whom we may with all confidence lift up our eyes to God and cry, "Abba, Father!" (8:15). And, "the Spirit Himself bears witness with our spirit," (8:16) through His powerful Word, "that we are children of God" (8:16). Yes, especially when our poor spirit is at the point of sinking into despair during temptation and suffering, does the Holy Spirit comfort our spirit that we are, in spite of all, truly God's beloved children. "And if children, then heirs," namely "heirs of God and fellow heirs with Christ," of eternal life (8:17) "provided we suffer with him, in order that we may be also glorified with him" (8:17).

Oh, Christians, consider this and walk in the Spirit. Walk as Christ's redeemed, as dear children of God, as living temples of the Holy Spirit, joyfully, ardently, and confidently through this poor life toward everlasting life! Walk in the Spirit!

Letter XX
The Deep Longing for the Great Glory Promised to the Justified Christians

Romans 8:18–27

We justified Christians and children of God must often endure much cross and suffering. But all our cross and suffering is Christ's cross. We suffer "with Christ," as was noted briefly in the last letter. Understand, that also the sufferings which we as human beings endure in common with all created beings on earth, must first pass through the hand of God, Who we might say, brings them first to the cross of Christ, immerses them into the blood and wounds of Christ, and so transforms them for us into a Christ-cross and Christian suffering, as He considers it good and wholesome for us. This holds true even of the sufferings which we bring upon ourselves by our own folly and intemperance of the flesh, as is so often the case. "Sufferings of this present time" (8:18) are also brought on us by the old evil foe, the devil, who dogs our steps, and by the world that hates and persecutes us Christians. This then is very precisely the cross of Christ, the cross which comes upon us for the sake of and because of our faith and confession of Christ. Even so, it causes us pain and suffering when for the sake of Christ we have to crucify our flesh. And finally, our heavenly Father also chastises and disciplines us especially for our eternal welfare, and that He does out of love for Jesus' sake. You see then that we have cross and suffering indeed, but it is all the cross of Christ.

And now, St. Paul himself, so highly experienced in cross-bearing suffering says, "I consider the sufferings of this present time are not worth comparing with the glory that is to be revealed to us" (8:18). We should feel about sufferings similarly. We, too, ought to reckon that all the sufferings of our short lifetime are nothing more than a speck of dust in the scales compared to the great glory which now already exists for us and which shall be revealed in us in that instant when the hour of Christ strikes. Let's keep a longing, sharp eye out for this wonderful event.

> Oh, shame, thou weary soul!
> Look forward to the goal.
> There joy waits thee.[6]

That is great, great and eternal glory indeed. And this, my friends, is what beckons to you in God's Word and promise. Take heart! For listen well, I've something more to tell you from God's Word! "For the creation waits with eager longing for the revealing of the sons of God" (8:19). All created things: animals, fish, birds, plants, flowers, vegetation of every sort, the sea, rivers, hills and valleys, sun, moon and stars—all creation waits as on tiptoes for God's children to be revealed in glory, waits for the time when all will see what God has prepared for us and what we really are and shall forever be. This anxious waiting of creation we, of course, do not observe with our physical eyes, even as the creation is not actually aware of it. But God's eyes see it clearly, God is very much aware of and concerned about it all.

> These great mysteries unsounded,
> Are by God alone expounded.[7]

"For the creation was subjected to futility" (8:20a), was given over to pitiable vanity and perishableness. Beautiful and wonderful as it was all created, and beautiful and wonderful as it still is, nature, as we know it, is being mauled, abused, and made to suffer in every which way by the gruesome course of death. This we can see all too clearly. No, creation was "not willingly" (8:20) by her own choice, subjected to this curse. She was subjected, and forcibly so by God, Who cursed her also after Adam's fall into sin. Her true and actual being struggles against it, for her actual and true being is pure life and loveliness.

---

[6] Wilhelm Arends, "Rise! To Arms! With Prayer Employ You," stanza 2.
[7] Johann Franck, "Soul, Adorn Yourself with Gladness," stanza 6.

But she was subjected "in hope" to the curse of death (8:20). Note it well, "the creation itself will be set free from its bondage to corruption" (8:21a) in which it now is. And not only will "the creation" be delivered, but she will also "obtain the freedom of the glory of the children of God" (8:21b). She will share in the great future liberty of God's children when these, delivered from all evil, shall be in purest and serenest glory of both body and soul. Then "the creation," the entire created universe with all its myriad forms of life and beauty, will be free from all evil and shimmer in pure eternal glory. Just like the bodies of God's children, so also all creation will rise out of dust and ashes, become new and be made heavenly in her manner and degree. God himself tells us this very thing in Isaiah 65:17, "For behold, I create new heavens and a new earth, and the former things shall not be remembered or come into mind." St. Peter also testifies and says, "According to his promise we are waiting for new heavens and a new earth in which righteousness dwells" (2 Pet. 3:13). And this he says, after he pointed out that on the day of God wherein the heavens being on fire shall be dissolved "the heavenly bodies will be burned up and dissolved" (2 Pet. 3:10). St. John echoes this very thing when he wrote, "Then I saw a new heaven and a new earth, for the first heaven and the first earth had passed away, and the sea was no more" (Rev. 21:1). Oh, how glorious all creation will then be!

And all this will be for us to heighten and increase our glorification. Keep your eye on that when you are in the depths of suffering and despair, my friend! Even now already we should so regard the created world about us, for we even now already know, see, and observe how she in all her countless voices groans and moans in longing for this hour. But by faith in God's Word we must bear in mind that such great moaning and groaning of nature is in reality an expression of anxious longing and waiting for the revelation in glory of God's children, in which nature also will share, all in order to magnify our glory and blessedness (8:22).

"And not only the creation," in its myriad forms, "but we ourselves," we Christians, moan and groan in ourselves waiting (8:23). Even though we "have the firstfruits of the Spirit" (8:23), and even though we have the Holy Spirit, the true God, and the great and mighty Comforter Himself as a firstfruits, earnest, down payment, and foretaste of the sum total of the great glory which

God has promised us and which we shall have, we still "groan inwardly" (8:23). Even though we have now already a piece of heaven and of the glory to carry about in ourselves, and even though we are by faith even now already fully aware of what glory we have to expect—we "grown inwardly" (8:23) and are burdened down with manifold sufferings of this present time. Who would possibly deny it? We painfully experience the cross constantly that lies on our backs. Many groans and sighs ascend from us to our God. God hears many a groan and anxious, plaintive whimpering and calling and screaming and begging and pleading that forces its way through to Him out of the sufferings of Christians everywhere. But how is it really? With us, there is in the midst of our groaning always a waiting. A waiting, born out of God's Word and the Holy Spirit, that is waiting "eagerly for adoption" as children of God; namely "the redemption of our bodies" (8:23) from all evil. This will occur on the blessed day in which we shall see and behold, fully have, and really enjoy what we now hope for in faith out of God's Word and promise.

Yes, then:

> Our God will free us
> From all our miseries
> From Satan and all evil
> From fear, anxieties
> From weeping and lamenting
> From illness, hurt and tears
> From sorrow and complaining
> Endured throughout our years.[8]

God has saved us through our Lord Jesus Christ and the Holy Spirit Who has brought us to faith, "For in this hope we were saved" (8:24). We do not as yet see this heavenly blessedness. That is why it is our *hope*. "Now hope that is seen is not hope. For who hopes for what he sees?" (8:24). "But if we hope for what we do not see," (8:25) then what do we do? "We wait for it with patience" (8:25). This longing and patient waiting for our adoption

---

[8] Johann Walter, "The Bridegroom Soon Will Call Us," stanza 7.

as children, the redemption of our bodies, is the Holy Spirit's blessed work in us through the Word of grace, the gospel.

But, dear Christians, I wish to tell you of yet another great sighing and groaning, which likewise arises from earth to heaven as it does out of the brute world and out of us, God's children. It is the groaning of the Holy Spirit. You can't believe it? Let me explain.

The sighing of God's people is and always will be a childlike pleading, "Deliver us from evil. Amen. Thou hast promised!" It's like that, isn't it? But we are weak, often so very, very weak that we can barely pray anymore. And we just do not know what we should pray nor how it is proper to pray under the oppressive circumstances. It seems the cross would almost crush us into the dust. And then also our praying does not fit, just isn't suitable to the great, glorious, heavenly, and unbreakable divine promises of deliverance which we can momentarily expect. If we at such times compare our praying to that for which we are praying—and, what is so most certainly promised to us and is so unbelievably great—then, we must be ashamed of our miserably inadequate praying. Our praying really ought to be a mighty prayer of rejoicing and thanksgiving because of the promised glory that awaits us, and for the patience and endurance which we still need so desperately in our present plight. But we are weak and our prayers so puny. Then the Holy Spirit has pity on us because of our weakness, becomes our Advocate, pleads our cause as only He can himself, "with groanings too deep for words" (8:26). The Holy Spirit dwells in us; we are His temple and dwelling. He loves us. Our misery and sighing affects Him deeply. He is truly concerned about our weakness, and He Himself moans in pleading compassion within us. Since He dwells within us, we may well notice something now and then of His praying within us. In time of deepest discouragements and greatest weakness we are aware of a decidedly strange power lifting us, and a sighing, calling, and pleading out of ourselves for our promised redemption. It is "the Spirit [who] helps us in our weakness," pleading our cause and coming to our aid "with groaning too deep for words" (8:26). Indeed, these groanings of the Holy Spirit that arise out of our inward selves and of which we are certainly aware, are unutterable to us. We just cannot put them in words. "And he who searches hearts knows what is the mind of the Spirit" (8:27), what He has in mind. He knows that the Holy Spirit comes to our aid as our Advocate in a manner pleasing to God. And this He does for all who are God's saints justified by faith in Christ. He, the Spirit of the Father, pleads and intercedes in all perfection in and out of us who are God's children. He, the Spirit of Christ, intercedes in fullest propriety for us, the redeemed of Christ. He Who is the Lord and Dispenser of glory, sighs and pleads for this heavenly glory in a manner fully commensurate to the grandeur of this glory. Surely, His pleading will be heard and granted! Be it day or night, sleeping or waking, also when our mind and reason at our last end fades away; yes, especially then, the Holy Spirit comes mightily to our aid with unutterable sighs and prayers for our redemption and promised heavenly glory. This is the deep longing for the great glory promised to the justified Christians.

LETTER XXI
THE JUSTIFIED CHRISTIAN'S ETERNAL DIVINE COMFORT UNDER THE CROSS

Romans 8:28–39

We, who by God's grace through faith in Christ have been justified and are God's children, love God. We do not love Him as we ought, nor as we would, but we do love Him. That is our new God-given nature. It's our mark of recognition. By it we are known and called both in heaven and on earth. We love our heavenly Father as His dear children. So we can, so we dare to, so we ought to, and so we do love him. We love Him in childlike confidence and reliance and trust that He will give us and do for us everything that is good and only good.

Therefore, when we must languish under and endure cross and suffering, we always add a "Yes, but..." and say, "We know that for those who love God all things work together for good" (8:28). We know that God, Who has caused us to love Him in such childlike trust and expectation of all that is only good—we know that He will surely not let our loving confidence and expectation fail us. And so we know that God, Who controls everything, lets all things serve our best—even our cross and suffering. "All things work together for good," (8:28) namely, that we stand fast in the faith and are finally safe in heaven. That *is* the best. To that end, God makes all things work together for us. To that end, our God makes all things work together with His powerful Word which is the one great means through which He works. To that best end He also makes our cross and suffering serve us. We *know* that. And this "knowing" throws a most wonderfully comforting light upon our cross and suffering.

This we *know*, I repeat. And this knowing we make altogether certain with the following God-breathed observation.

Those people who love God, who therefore are Christians, they became Christians because of the fact that they are the called ones of God and because they have been called to Christ through the gospel. This calling also includes being called to the fellowship of believers, the communion of saints, to the great unnumbered throng of Christians, and to God's beloved Christian church. But, understand this correctly! Through this calling, God has not merely invited and summoned them to become Christians. No, through this calling, God has actually made them Christians, actually brought them to Christ, to the fellowship of believers and saints and children of God, to the vast throng of Christians, to God's beloved Christian church. In a nutshell, through this calling God not only told them of and gave them His Holy Spirit's strength that they should convert themselves, but through this calling God actually and truly did convert them. This calling, then, did become powerful and effective in them and did accomplish its purpose.

Why? Why did this calling accomplish its purpose on those who became Christians? Was the cause or the motive for it perhaps in them? Were they perhaps in themselves different somehow from the many others who did not respond to the calling, the beckoning of God? Were they more inclined than others to come to Christ? Did they have a different or better attitude to God's calling? No, not at all! None of these. They are, as we know, by nature flesh and fleshly minded (1 Cor. 2:14). As such, they neither receive nor accept the things of the Sprit of God, because they are foolishness to them. They cannot know them and are enemies of God like all others. Why then did this calling accomplish its purpose in those who became Christians? If the reason was not in themselves, where then? In God alone. God called them "according to his purpose" (8:28). God on purpose and with premeditation, determined to convert them through His calling. And so they were converted through this calling of God. But that does not say that those who are not converted by God's calling, are not converted "according to God's purpose," that God had a secret purpose *not* to convert them, that it then was in God that they were not converted. No, the reason why they are not converted, that was only and alone in themselves. But those who are converted by the calling of God, were converted "according to God's purpose," according to God's eternal purpose and determination which cannot fail or be overthrown.

Now then, if God by His grace for Jesus' sake has made such a loving determination and has carried it into effect to the point that He has actually made them believing Christians who love Him, and made them heirs of eternal life, then it surely is absolutely certain that He would now make all things—including their cross and suffering—work together so that they would cling to the faith and finally be safe in heaven.

"For those whom he foreknew" (8:29), He selected or chose for Himself in such great love and for whose sake God made that aforedescribed eternal determination, those "he also predestined to be conformed to the image of his Son," (8:29) that they should be transfigured in eternal glory like His Son our Lord Jesus Christ is transfigured and glorified. All this so that Christ "might be the firstborn among many brothers" (8:29). All this so that Christ might be the The Numero Uno, The Prince among many brothers. Yes, brothers, for He, the eternal, great Son of God became man and still is now and will be eternally man; God and man, The God-Man, Immanuel. This I tell you straight out of God's Word. Isn't it now again absolutely certain that God lets "all things work together for good" (8:28) to those who love Him? Yes their cross and sufferings too, that they remain rooted in the faith and finally be safe in heaven with Him.

And now, dear Christians, pay close attention! "Those whom he predestined he also called," (8:30) in their lifetime and brought them to faith. Well, didn't God call you, bring you to faith? "And those whom he called he also justified" (8:30). Didn't God justify you? "And those whom he justified he also glorified" (8:30). Not only are they already glorified, but he also gave them their glorification as a divinely certified possession. He will most certainly give you eternal glory. He will most certainly make all things, even your cross and trials, work together for good to you, so that you hold to the faith and finally be safe in heaven. Why, even now already you see yourselves well along in this process to work out His gracious and loving predetermination, to bring His eternal purpose to crowning completion and perfection for you, since—as you know—he has already converted and justified you.

"What then shall we say to these things? If God is for us," so powerfully and invincibly on our side, "who can be against us" (8:31) to hurt or destroy us? "He who did not spare his own Son but gave him up for us all, how will he not also with him graciously give us all things?" (8:32). "All things" includes all that is good, truly good, the very best, yes, even everlasting salvation. And we Christians are the chosen ones of God, the elect. We are those whom God already in eternity predetermined and predestined and in His great love chose as His own. We are the ones whom God preordained and chose beforehand, and whom He, therefore, has already called and justified and designated as bona fide heirs of glory. We are the ones for whom God makes all things work for good, that we remain in the faith and finally reach the eternal goal of glory. That being true, and it surely is, "Who shall bring any charge against God's elect?" (8:33). Who will accuse us before God on account of our sins and so wedge himself between us and God's grace and gift? Would the devil do it? Or the world? Or our own heart and conscience? Or the Law? "It is God who justifies" (8:33). And "who is to condemn?" (8:34). Who could do that? "Christ Jesus is the one who died—more than that, who was raised—who is at the right hand of God, who indeed is interceding for us" (8:34) with the bloody purchase price of His cross, with His perfect righteousness, and with His constant pleading on our behalf that can never be refused. "Who shall separate us from the love of Christ" (8:35) from the great and fervent love that God has for us in Christ? "Shall tribulation, or distress, or persecution, or famine, or nakedness, or danger, or sword?" (8:35). Or any cross or trial whatever? It is true, of course, we Christians have many trials. The hatred of Satan and of the world against Christ falls on us who are His. It is with us as it is written, "For your sake we are being killed all the day long; we are regarded as sheep to be slaughtered" (8:36). But shall all of this or some of it, perhaps, overwhelm us, that we should fall from the faith and lose Christ and His salvation? Oh no! "In all these things we are more than conquerors" (8:37). How come? Are we so strong and rugged? On no! We are more than conquerors "through him who loved us" (8:37), our Lord Jesus Christ who with His ever-constant love runs to our side and supports us against all comers, so that nothing, "will be able to separate us from the love of God which is in Christ Jesus our Lord" (8:39).

Treasure this securely in your hearts, you Christians! And then let each one very neatly and most properly in calm faith and with joyous song say, "I am going to be forever safe in heaven!" "For I am sure that neither death nor life, nor angels nor rulers, nor things present nor things to come, nor powers, nor height nor depth, nor anything else in all creation, will be able to separate us from the love of God in Christ Jesus our Lord" (8:38–39).

This is the certainty of our salvation. This is grounded and founded upon God's Word of grace. It is grounded on the love of God in Christ Jesus, Who has chosen us in eternity and leads us unerringly on the way ordained by God through everything to everlasting salvation. This certainty of our salvation is not a knowledge which is to be calculated and reckoned by fleshly hearts outside of God's promises, but it is a certainty which the Spirit-produced faith grounds on God's sure promises. Everything that God says He says only for that faith alone.

This is the justified Christian's eternal divine comfort under the cross and trials of life.

Letter XXII
Not All Who Are Descended from Israel Belong to Israel

Romans 9:1–13

We have heard about the Jews in these letters before already. We will hear more of them now and more in depth, to be sure. As you know, the Jews were known as God's chosen people for 2000 years and their race never did disappear. They are still here. For this reason, the Holy Spirit has much to say concerning them in Holy Scripture and especially in the Epistle to the Romans. And as we place this before ourselves for earnest consideration, we who are Christians will learn much wholesome doctrine and teaching.

St. Paul writes, "I am speaking the truth in Christ—I am not lying; my conscience bears me witness in the Holy Spirit—that I have great sorrow and unceasing anguish in my heart. For I could wish that I myself were accursed and cut off from Christ for the sake of my brothers, my kinsmen according to the flesh" (9:1–3). It was with the Jews that these words had to do. For what was the state of affairs with them? What moved Paul to write like this? The great majority of Jews had categorically rejected Christ, the Messiah, the only Savior Who had been preached to them by the apostles. In all countries wherever Jews lived and where the apostles' preaching was heard, the Jews joined in the horrible Passover festival scream of their brothers, "Away with him, away with him, crucify him!" (John 19:15). And ever since then, they have done the same; yes, and they still do. They were and are today anathema, a curse, an indignation of God because they were far from Christ and still are. They made themselves what they are, because they rejected Christ, the only Savior. That caused Paul the apostle constant pain and anguish beyond measure. He asserts this as a Christian. Paul assures his readers that this was a genuine pain and anguish that he knew in his Spirit-controlled conscience. Yes, the thought had entered his mind, as once to Moses also, that he could wish himself to be banned from Christ in place of those who were his brothers according to the flesh, according to race and origin. And not only because the Jews were his relatives after the flesh, but there had been given to them so much and such great things! From Jacob who also was named Israel, they inherited the name of honor, Israelites. They had received the right of children. They were chosen as the people of God and made such in preference to all nations of the earth. "The glory" (9:4) had been given them. In the cloud, which on their journey through the wilderness went with them, dark in daylight, glowing ahead of them at night, in that *shechinah* the cloud that settled in the tabernacle and later in the temple and was called "the glory of the Lord," God had revealed and assured them of His gracious and constant presence. That covenant, that oft-repeated contract, God had made with them, that He would be their God and they His people. The Law of God had been revealed and entrusted to them; the true and right worship had been established among them; the promises of the Christ were given them in richest abundance through the prophets. Abraham, Isaac, and Jacob; these great ones were their fathers. And the Christ of God Himself is descended from them according to His human nature; the Christ, "who is God over all, blessed forever. Amen" (9:5). Where was there ever such a glorious people as Israel? And now—now, they were and still are banned from Christ! That moved, shook, and grieved the Apostle Paul beyond measure. And it is, in very truth, shocking and astonishing to say the least!

But that does not say, nor dare it be so construed, as though the Word of God which He spoke concerning Israel, and God's promise which He made to Israel had become null and void. Which word? Which promise? The Word and the promise that Israel should be helped, that Israel should be saved. This Word, this promise had been made to Israel constantly and in every possible way and with great might, clarity, and exactness. And this certainly is, by far, the greatest of all the advantages that had been given to Israel. And this Word, this promise, I say, did not fail. But how? Were not the Jews in greatest majority, banished from Christ? And, isn't that true even today yet? True! And yet, God's Word and promise that Israel shall be helped and saved through Christ is not null and void, did not fail. But how shall we then understand and explain this?

Listen! "Not all who are descended from Israel belong to Israel" (9:6) in God's sight. Not all who are Abraham's seed and because they are Abraham's seed, because they descended from Abraham, are for that reason also children, genuine, true children of Abraham in God's eyes. Not the entire fleshly and outward Israel is that Israel which God had in mind, when He gave to Israel the Word and promise, that he shall be helped through Christ, that he shall be saved through Christ. God had an Israel in mind which was descended from Abraham not only according to the flesh, but one which was descended from Abraham also according to the Spirit, the Israel which was and is and always will be truly Israel; God's people in truth.

Not all the natural, physical children of Abraham were children and heirs of the great promise of salvation through Christ. Only those are who are in the likeness of Abraham in Spirit and faith. These, these alone, are the Israel to which God gave His Word and His promise of salvation through Christ. And such there always were, such are here now, and such there will always be, even though there will be only a small number of them. And to these God's Word and promise remain firm. You Christians know this, of course. That is a matter clearly set forth and demonstrated in Holy Scripture in many places. However, we must, at this point, bear this well in mind.

This truth that "not all who are descended from Israel belong to Israel" (9:6); namely, that the promise of salvation through Christ is not meant for the entire physical Israel, but only for that spiritual Israel which lay hidden in Old Testament times in the physical Israel and which stepped forth out of Israel in the times of the New Testament, is now typified and illustrated in the history of the ancestors of Israel.

Abraham had two sons: Ishmael and Isaac. Ishmael was born according to the flesh, according to the usual order of nature. Isaac, however, was born contrary to the order of nature, according to the miraculously fulfilled promise given in such a wonderful manner to Abraham. That was indeed a wonderful word of promise that Abraham received from God in his great age, "About this time next year I will return, and Sarah shall have a son" (9:9). And Sarah's womb had already become barren. And miraculously, a year later the promise was fulfilled. Sarah gave Abraham a son, Isaac. And later God told Abraham, "Though Isaac shall your offspring be named" (9:7). In other words, that people promised to Abraham in which the Christ was to become a human being, was not to come from Ishmael born according to the flesh, but alone from Isaac, the one born according to the promise. So then, the people promised to Abraham should call Isaac only, alone, and altogether the founder of their race, their ancestor. From this, God would and we too should explain, "not all who are descended from Israel belong to Israel" (9:6). The children of God whom God recognizes as a people and to whom He has given the promise of salvation in Christ are not the physical children (those of fleshly lineage). On the contrary, only the children of the promise are counted as "seed." What does this mean? Only they in Israel who are born of the promise, who were begotten of the Word of promise, the gospel of Christ, who were born again and made believers, only they are reckoned as "seed of Abraham," as the true children of Abraham, the true Israel. And only to them has God given the promise of eternal life through the Christ. That is what it means. That is what we, according to God's will, understand out of this historical event, which, in itself, obviously dealt only with the secular and physical Israel and its origin.

But not only is it so with this historical event. "And not only so, but also when Rebekah had conceived children by one man, our forefather Isaac, though they were not yet born and had done nothing either good or bad" (9:10–11a), "She was told, 'The older will serve the younger'" (9:12). Meaning, the first born shall become subservient to the younger one. And that means, of course, that not the first born, but the last born shall be the founder of the promised race, Israel, from which the Christ, the Lord should come. God says that also through the prophet, "Jacob I loved, but Esau I hated" (9:13). Which means, I have made Jacob to be the founder of the promised people of Israel, elected according to my own pleasure; I have not elected Esau for it, but have rejected him. It has not been my pleasure that Esau should be my choice. And why? Ah, Christians, this is as God had intended it beforehand to be; simply so that it would be and remain precisely so. Namely, that it would not be a matter of human works and human advantages but a matter of the free grace of Him Who may call to such a position whom He wills. Also from this we should understand that "not all who are descended from Israel belong to Israel" (9:6).

So, indeed it is. But mark this well! By this it is by no means said that it comes from God and from God's choice and design, when someone does not become a true Israelite. It is not because God does not will to call and convert him, but because he will not let himself be called and converted, that and that alone is the reason why one does not become a true Israelite. So then, not all are Israelites who are of Israel, even as also all are not Christians who are outwardly in Christendom. Mark it well!

LETTER XXIII
"SO THEN HE HAS MERCY ON WHOMEVER HE WILLS, AND HE HARDENS WHOMEVER HE WILLS."

Romans 9:14–18

Today we shall try to understand this much-misunderstood Word of God.

I just finished saying that it is not those, who are Israelites after the flesh, who are therefore also the true Israel of God to whom God has given the promise of eternal life through Christ. Not any sort of human advantage or preference, not any sort of human doing, work, or attitude of merit makes anyone a true Israelite. No, God alone does that. And, to be sure, God does that by His own free choice, by nothing except His fore-determined purpose of grace. That God alone does. He, out of free grace, calls to Christ and converts whomever out of Israel He wills.

What shall we say to this? Surely it is not that God is unjust. Surely there is not that injustice in God which He condemns in human beings when He says, "He who justifies the wicked and he who condemns the righteous are both alike an abomination to the LORD" (Prov. 17:15). Never! God forbid! Such thoughts we dare not even entertain. God is Righteousness itself. This is the first point we want to settle. And that statement made in the last letter shall stand fully and completely because that statement is firmly grounded in Scripture which is God's own Word. That is the second point we want to make. For how do we read in Exodus 33:17–20? Moses, that great man and servant of God, had just received this assurance from God, "You have found favor in my sight, and I know you by name" (Exod. 33:17). And now, he became bold and said to God, "Please show me your glory" (Exod.

33:18). This request God denied him sharply. Why? Because Moses wanted for himself a preference granted to no living man, to behold God in His glory. But God did say, "I will make all my goodness pass before you and will proclaim before you my name 'The LORD" (Exod. 33:19a). That was grace enough, that was saving grace. However, in this passage of God's glory before Moses, God gave Moses to understand, "I will have mercy on whom I have mercy, and I will have compassion on whom I have compassion" (9:15). Moses was to understand clearly that he also should, for no conceivable reason, have not the slightest preferential claim on God's grace and mercy. He was to know that God gives His grace and mercy to whom He gives it, to whom He will. From this surely it is clear: if anyone out of Israel is called and converted and brought to the true Israel by God, if God gives the promise of everlasting life in Christ to anyone, it was not because of "human will or exertion, but on God, who has mercy" (9:16). Therefore, it is not some human excellence or advantage, not some human doing, work, conduct, or merit that makes a person a true Israelite; never, that God alone does. And, what is more, God does that according to His own free choice, according to His own purpose motivated only and alone by His grace. God does this alone, in that He out of free grace alone calls and converts to Christ, whomever He wills out of Israel.

If it depended on someone's "will or exertion" (9:16) that he be converted and brought to the true Israel of God and saved, then, obviously, it would no longer be pure grace. And, dear fellow Christian, you surely know that it is grace alone. Therefore, this comes alone from God and His grace and His gracious purpose and choice. Consider also this: as soon as anyone has this "will or exertion" in the true sense of the Word, then he already is a true Israelite, then he already is converted and made an heir of salvation. A person is not made a true Israelite because he had this "will or exertion" in himself; on the contrary, this "will or exertion is found in a person now, because he was made by God a true Israelite out of pure mercy, before he had this "will or exertion" (9:16).

God is not unjust because He will not permit Himself to be influenced to make His choice by a person's conduct. That is now proven with two basic reasons: first, God cannot be unjust (that is out of the question!); second, it is proven by God's own statements in Holy Scripture that He deals that way. That surely is proof enough.

And now we must consider the other side of the question. When God does not make someone a true Israelite, but lets him remain in unbelief, in hardness of heart and damnation, is He then perhaps unjust? Also, here we must say, "Perish the very thought!" Also in this, all thoughts of God being unjust must remain far from our minds. Also in this, we dare never forget that God is Righteousness itself. And also for this, we have the Holy Scriptures, which expressly say that God operates like that.

The particular Scripture that I mean is the one which deals with Pharaoh; that godless Pharaoh who so plagued and suppressed the people of Israel. To this Pharaoh God sent His servant Moses with the command that he, Pharaoh, should permit the children of Israel to leave Egypt. But Pharaoh set himself against God's will with all the stiffneckedness and hardness of heart he had in him. So God spoke to him through Moses, "But for this purpose I have raised you up, to show you my power, so that my name may be proclaimed in all the earth" (Exod. 9:16). So, here Holy Scripture, God's Word, says what? It says God had raised up Pharaoh, that means God let him rise up and rise up as he did, namely as a stiffnecked and hardened despiser of God and enemy of God's people. Scripture also says why God permitted Pharaoh to rise up like that, namely for this purpose, "that I might show my power in you" (9:17), more specifically, His power to destroy. And Scripture says that God wanted to show His power in Pharaoh for this purpose, "that my name might be proclaimed in all the earth" (9:17). That all the earth should see that God destroys His enemies, but that He in doing so, saves His own people, in order that in this way, in all nations, many people should come to the right and true knowledge of God.

So then, God permitted Pharaoh to remain in unbelief. Yes, God hardened his heart, as Scripture expressly and repeatedly reports, in order to destroy and damn him. Hardening of the heart, you see, is the first step, in this world, of damnation. He whose heart is hardened by God, he will also be damned. And God wanted to leave Pharaoh in unbelief and wanted to harden his heart and destroy and damn him. But now, mark this well and take this to heart! Here God did *not* say, "With whomsoever I am angry, with him I am angry and whomsoever I harden and destroy, him I harden and destroy." Here Scripture does *not* say that it does not depend on someone's "will or exertion" but on God's wrath and His delight to show wrath, when someone stays in unbelief, is hardened and damned. Here one dare not say that human doing, work, behavior, and deserts do not bring it on when someone does not belong to God's people and is saved. Here one dare not say that God works it according to his free choice and according to his purpose influenced entirely and totally by his delight to show wrath. Here one dare not say that God lets remain in unbelief, hardens, and damns whomever he wills, without letting himself be influenced and induced to do so by his behavior. No, "Say to them, As I live, declares the Lord GOD, I have no pleasure in the death of the wicked, but that the wicked turn from his way and life; turn back, turn back from your evil ways, for why will you die, O house of Israel?" (Ezek. 33:11). God permitted Pharaoh to remain in unbelief because Pharaoh wanted to remain in unbelief, regardless! God hardened Pharaoh because Pharaoh had hardened himself first. God had worked on Pharaoh constantly and earnestly with the sincere intention of converting him, through word and deed, great signs and miracles. All was useless. Constantly, Pharaoh opposed himself to God's Word and works of wonder. Constantly, Pharaoh hardened himself. So, finally God's judgment came down upon him. Which judgment? Now Pharaoh shall remain in his unbelief, now God willed it to leave him in unbelief. Now Pharaoh should be hardened, now God wanted to harden him. And now God hardened him. God now gave him over completely to his own evil heart, which, of course, of its own self and its own strength neither wanted to nor could convert itself. God now quit working on him through His Holy Spirit, without Whom no one can convert himself. Now God set before him one opportunity after the other to confirm his hardness of heart and let it come to its highest point of ripeness. And finally God destroyed and damned him. It was God's judgment, God's righteous judgment, therefore, that God permitted Pharaoh to remain in unbelief, hardened, and damned him. This judgment God inflicted upon Pharaoh and wanted to inflict upon Pharaoh, because Pharaoh did not want to convert himself but had hardened himself.

And here now is our Bible verse, "So then he has mercy on whomever he wills, and he hardens whomever he wills" (9:18). Do you understand that one now, Christians? God has mercy on whom He will. God converts and makes into a genuine Israelite and heir of eternal salvation without the man's behavior, which cannot, in any way influence Him. It is altogether according to His free grace and purpose, election, and plan. And God hardens whom He will. God will let one remain in unbelief and harden him and damn him, who through persistent rebellion and through self-hardening, made God will it so, pulled down in himself this judgment of God.

This is how we must understand this Bible verse. In this manner we are to know God. This is the way God revealed Himself to us. That God deals in this way with us, of this we should be sure. For as God deals with Israel, so He also deals with us, as Pharaoh's example points out, who also did not belong to Israel.

LETTER XXIV
"WHY DOES HE STILL FIND FAULT? FOR WHO CAN RESIST HIS WILL?"

Romans 9:19–29

It was said in the last letter that God "has mercy on whomever he wills" (9:18). God converts and makes true Israelites and heirs of eternal life without a person being able in the slightest to influence Him to do so, totally according to His free grace and provision, election and intention. And God hardens whom He will. God wills to leave in unbelief, to harden and condemn him who by persistent opposition and self-hardening made God so to will it, and who so draws God's judgment down upon himself.

Here human reason loudly protests and objects saying: "Why does he still find fault? For who can resist his will" (9:19)? What is here meant? It is said somewhat like this: it cannot be true that God and God's will has anything to do with the fact that a person remains in unbelief and is hardened. It is of course true that many people remain in unbelief by their own fault, harden themselves, and are lost. But, that God finally wills it to abandon them in unbelief, harden them, and then actually does harden them, that cannot be true. For then, "Why does he still find fault? Who can resist his will?" (9:19). And now, it also is said that God converts whom He will without taking a person's behavior or conduct into consideration even one small bit. God should convert whom He wills altogether according to His free grace, provision, election, and intention. Ah, then, why does God not convert all people? Why then does He let it go on and on so far with many that they harden themselves? If that's the way it is, then surely it would depend on God's will!

And "why does he still find fault?" He faults, He blames the hardened ones, doesn't He? How could He do this, if everything depended on His will? For who can resist His will? This is the objection one hears.

Before I give the answer to the objection which it deserves, I too, shall first attempt to produce several similar protests out of my own reason. Namely these: how about the fall of Satan and his angels? Didn't God have the power to hinder that? The power He had, of course. It was not contingent upon God's power, obviously. Why then did God not prevent the fall and everlasting damnation of Satan and his angels? If it was not a lack of power with God, then it must have been a matter of His will. But it if were, "why does he still find fault?" Who can resist God's will? And what of the fall of our first parents, Adam and Eve? Didn't God have the power to prevent Satan from misleading them so they would not fall into sin? He also knew how much misery, death, and damnation would come of that, didn't He? Of power to prevent that, there surely was no lack for the Almighty, to be sure. Was it then dependent on His will that He did not prevent that? Obviously, of course! "Why does he still find fault? For who can resist His will?" (9:19). Many baptized children God permits to die in their baptismal grace and so saves them. Others He lets live and they fall away and are lost eternally. That happens every so often. Why does God, Who sees everything long before it happens, why does He not let these, too, die in their baptismal grace and save them? He is Lord over life and death, isn't He? It must depend upon His will. But, "Why does he still find fault? For who can resist His will?" (9:19).

Christian friends! With all these objections and remonstrances one enters upon a domain upon which absolutely no one may dare to enter. What domain is that? Upon the domain of the unrevealed majesty and the incomprehensible will of the sovereign God. Upon this domain our faith would not presume to enter, for our faith depends alone on God's revealed Word. Upon this domain only our puny, miserable, blind, corrupt, over-inflated, impertinent, and insolent reason wants to enter, and there dispute with the divine majesty and master it and wrangle, yes, put to shame, make helpless, and bankrupt the omniscient God Himself. And now, to return again to the actual objection under consideration, one would like to say somewhat like this, "God wants to save us human beings through Christ (right). And God has established an order in which we are to be saved, namely that of faith in Jesus Christ (right). That we will be saved in this established order, He has given us His Word and the power of His Holy Spirit (right)."

That's it! Now He leaves us to ourselves and to our fate. Now He waits to see how we make do. Now, as to the rest of it, He draws back into Himself all His might and His will. Now, He interferes further no more whatever. No, He who believes will be saved. He who does not believe will be damned. For if God's might and God's will were still involved, one way or the other, with those who will be converted and saved, or with those who will be hardened and damned, "Why does he still find fault? For who can resist His will?" (9:19). Then surely He Himself would be the cause of the ultimate unbelief and damnation.

So, man would dispute with the Divine Majesty and find fault with Him. But, what is the answer that then comes from the Divine Majesty? This, "But who are you, O man?" (9:20). What is meant? It means, "Yes. Indeed, yes there is a divine majesty and a sovereign will of God, against which nothing can possibly oppose." And this, "But who are you, O man, to answer back to God?" (9:20). And this, "Will what is molded say to its molder, 'Why have you made me like this?' Has the potter no right over the clay, to make out of the same lump one vessel for honorable use and another for dishonorable use? (9:20–21). So the divine majesty flashes such a one down who would want to dispute, find fault with, and bring it to shame and disgrace. As though it would say, "Oh yes, *you* impertinent wretch, I am here, and My will is here. And I shall clear up nothing to you. No, I shall maintain Myself in My unapproachable greatness and boundless perfection of power and might."

Whether we shall ever, even in the life to come, be able to fully comprehend that majesty and sovereign will of God, that I don't know. I doubt it. In any case, we shall then in overpowering awe and with perfect discernment know that God is right, just, and good. We shall then worship and glorify His divine majesty. But this I do know, that here in this world we dare not occupy ourselves in any way with this majesty and with this profound, sovereign will of God. In this life on earth, we are to occupy ourselves only with the revealed God and with the revealed will of God. That will not delude or disappoint us. We should never think that behind this revealed will of God there may still be that other sovereign will of God's majesty, possibly making the revealed will of God unreliable and void. Do you hear? God's sovereign will of divine majesty exists, is a reality. But you, Christians, have absolutely nothing in the least to do with that because that will just has not been revealed. And it does not contradict the revealed will. Yes, do you hear that?

Therefore, get your mind and eyes off that unrevealed but hidden majesty of the great God, and look all the more closely into the revealed Word, Holy Scripture, and into the history of God's ways and dealings with Israel related therein. From that you will learn to know God, His will, His way of dealing and His doing. There you will see that God, times beyond number, had the greatest and the most just cause to vent His wrath and let loose His destroying fury upon these people. How fickle, traitorous, headstrong, forever uncircumcised in hearts and ears, forever resisting the Holy Ghost, forever hardening themselves they are! He did finally want to let His wrath explode upon them and let them experience His destroying fury, as He threatened to thousands of times. But, what happened? Even though He wanted to do that, He nevertheless in great patience and longsuffering endured these "vessels of wrath prepared for destruction" (9:22). They had repeatedly made themselves fit and worthy to be destroyed, made themselves fully overripe for destruction and damnation, yet God over and over again worked on them in most earnest mercy and pity to convert them and make them truly His people. This He did throughout Old Testament times; He did it when He sent them Christ; so He did when He had the apostles preach to them even though they had rejected Christ Himself and crucified Him. Finally, the great Judgment did come; namely, the destruction of Jerusalem and the scattering abroad of the Jews among all nations. Yet even in this scattering abroad of the Jews, God exercised longsuffering on these hardened people. And in this longsuffering patience with these hardened people, these "vessels of wrath," God also had this constantly in mind, "To make known the riches of his glory for vessels of mercy, which he has prepared beforehand for glory" (9:23). "To make known the riches of His glorious grace to the vessels of mercy," namely, to His chosen ones who at that time were living in unbelief and among the great number of unbelievers and still do today. These He wanted to rescue from unbelief and out of the great number of unbelievers and still does today. Whom He wanted to fill with His mercy and still does today. Whom He, according to His eternal decree, had prepared to be in glory and for whom He before the world began prepared the kingdom of glory. His great hands reached out for these throughout those many years of His patience with the hardened people searching and recovering some—if only a few— even as they still search for and find some today among the Jewish people. But now, when you consider this well, you Christians, would you then want to dispute with God and say, "Why does he still find fault? For who can resist His will?" (9:19). Oh no, you would not! In His firm revealed Word you see how God would so gladly save both the "vessels of wrath" as well as the "vessels of mercy." Knowing that as we do, let us be content with it!

We see then, that God did achieve His objective with "the vessels of mercy," namely, with His chosen elect ones. He called and converted us Christians. What is more, God gathered us together to His true and real people not only from out of the Jewish people, but also out of the Gentiles. Yes, out of the Gentiles also. He wants it that way. "As indeed he says in Hosea, 'Those who were not my people I will call "my people," and her who was not beloved I will call "beloved."' 'And in the very place where it was said to them, "you are not my people," there they will be called "sons of the living God."'" (9:25–26). But also out of these Jews who lay so hopelessly in unbelief God always gathers in some, of course only some, only a remnant, like a drop out of an emptied bucket. Yes, also from out of the Jews, I say, God gathers always some to His true people whom He saves. Yes, that He wants to do. For His prophet Isaiah calls out over Israel, "Though the number of the sons of Israel be as the sand of the sea, only a remnant of them will be saved" (9:27). True, only a remnant. For Isaiah continues and says, "for the Lord will carry out his sentence upon the earth fully and without delay" (9:28). The Lord will finish His account with the Jewish nation on earth and put an end to it quickly "in righteousness," so all will see He dealt with these hardened ones in total fairness in the destruction of Jerusalem, AD 70. It goes as Isaiah said, "If the Lord of hosts had not left us offspring, we would have been like Sodom and become like Gomorrah" (9:29).

Had God not rescued a few out of Israel to be His people and the true seed of Abraham, we would have been altogether like Sodom and Gomorrah. Isaiah says that quite plainly.

So it is, indeed. No, we should not look into the blinding majesty of God. If we do, we shall suffer shipwreck of our faith and shall dispute and wrangle with God and say, "Why does he still find fault? For who can resist His will?" (9:19). No! We should look into the revealed Word of God and in reverence, love, and confidence find our rest and repose there. That will not betray or cheat us to be sure. Amen!

Letter XXV
The Faith of the Gentiles and the Unbelief of the Jews

Romans 9:30–10:21

Yes, God gathers for Himself a people out of Israel which believes in the Savior and is saved. But this people of God in Israel, compared to the great multitude of Israel, is only a remnant, a leftover, one might say. The great mass of Israel is hardened in unbelief and has succumbed to eternal destruction.

"What shall we say, then?" (9:30a). How does one explain that the great mass of Israel is so hardened in unbelief? Like this, "That Gentiles who did not pursue righteousness" (9:30a), who had no intention at all to fulfill God's will and Law, but served only their carnal lusts, these "have attained it, that is, a righteousness that is by faith" (9:30b). For in a manner totally unsought by them, the gospel of Christ was brought to them and by God's grace they were converted. "But that Israel who pursued a law that would lead to righteousness," (9:31) being intent upon fulfilling God's will and Law, offered some resistance to their fleshly lusts in considerable measure (I am not now speaking of those Jews who had become altogether like the godless Gentiles), but Israel "did not succeed in reaching that law" (9:31). Why not? "Because they did not pursue it by faith" this perfect righteousness which alone avails before God in Christ, but intended to gain it "as if it were based on works" (9:32). They had the gospel of Christ. But in their work-righteous and self-righteous mind and heart, "They have stumbled over the stumbling stone, as it is written, 'Behold, I am laying in Zion a stone of stumbling, and a rock of offense; and whoever believes in him will not be put to shame.'" (9:32–33). The result? They did not gain the righteousness that alone avails before

God. They ended in disaster. And that's the way it has been with Israel through all times and still is today.

"Brothers, my heart's desire and prayer to God for them is that they may be saved. For I bear them witness that they have a zeal for God, but not according to knowledge" (10:1–2). They do not recognize but misjudge the righteousness which God gives and which avails before God. Instead, they try to set up their own righteousness and "did not submit to God's righteousness," which alone is valid and acceptable with God (10:3). This righteousness is declared and offered to them in the Old Testament, likewise in the New Testament. But they will have nothing of it. And there just is no other in existence. "For Christ is the end of the law for righteousness to everyone who believes" (10:4). Christ puts an end to the Law which is impossible for us to bear, by fulfilling it in our stead and by extinguishing its curse. And then Christ extends to us His righteousness so earned by Him. He alone will be declared righteous by God who accepts Christ and Christ's righteousness, who puts his trust in Christ.

How is it then with the righteousness which comes out of the Law? "For Moses writes about the righteousness that is based on the law, that the person who does the commandments shall live by them" (10:5). So then, through the Law a person becomes righteous before God and is saved when he actually and perfectly does the Law. But no man can do that. Therefore, by the works of the Law no man becomes righteous.

How is it, then, with the righteousness which comes from Christ by faith? To have that, we have to do nothing whatsoever. With that it's simply, "'Do not say in your heart, "Who will ascend into heaven?" ' (that is, to bring Christ down) 'or "Who will descend into the abyss?" ' (that is, to bring Christ up from the dead." (10:6–7). No, no! You need not be anxiously concerned or worried in the least how you want to find Christ, His righteousness, and salvation.

> Ye need not toil or languish, Nor ponder day and night
> How in the midst of anguish, Ye draw Him by your might.
> He comes, He comes all willing, Moved by his love alone,

Your woes and troubles stilling; For all to him are known.[9]

Christ has already come, He has already made us righteous and saved us by his death and resurrection. And now He comes through His Word and the Holy Spirit, places Himself with His righteousness so gained for us into our hearts for us to put our confidence of faith into it and into our mouths for us to joyfully praise and glorify Him for it all. That is the reason why He says it here like this, "'The word is near you, in your mouth and in your heart' (that is, the word of faith that we proclaim)" (10:8). This is the Word about Christ which we Christians believe and confess. Oh, how near is Christ, His righteousness dearly purchased and salvation to you! Oh, how altogether certainly and securely is Christ, His righteousness and salvation your very own! For, listen, "If you confess with your mouth that Jesus is Lord and believe in your heart that God raised him from the dead, you will be saved" (10:9). For with the faith of the heart one grasps Christ for righteousness with which one stands acquitted and innocent before God, and with the mouth one confesses Him as the One Who saved us.

Oh truly, how altogether surely and securely you possess Christ and the righteousness which avails before God and heaven itself! And how absolutely nothing whatsoever is there for you to work, to do, and to have! You have only by faith to put your confidence in that which has already been given to you and you can with loudest praises glorify God. How foolish, how outrageous it is if one would yet with his own works, with works of the Law, attempt to gain that, as the Jews do!

"For Scripture says, 'Everyone who believes in him will not be put to shame'" (10:11). "Everyone," it says. For, as you know, it matters not whether one is a Jew or a Greek, a Gentile, by race. "For the same Lord is Lord of all, bestowing his riches on all who call on him. For 'everyone who calls on the name of the Lord'" by faith "'will be saved'" (10:12b–13) says the prophet Joel. Oh you Jews, you Jews, why don't you want to believe?

Now this, of course, is true, "How then will they call on him in whom they have not believed? And how are they to believe in him

---

[9] Paul Gerhardt, "O Lord, How Shall I Meet Thee," stanza 7.

of whom they have never heard? And how are they to hear him without someone preaching? And how are they to preach unless they are sent?" (10:14–15a). But, what does Isaiah prophesy? "How beautiful are the feet of those who preach the good news!" (10:15b). This prophecy has been fulfilled. The Lord has sent His disciples into all the world and also to the Jews, with the gospel. "But they have not all obeyed the gospel" (10:16a). There's the problem! "For Isaiah says, 'Lord, who has believed what he has heard from us?'" (10:16b).

So, then, how is it with the Jews? Faith, as you know, can come only from the preaching of the gospel. The preaching of the gospel, however, is only by the Word and command of God, where God sends His messengers and preachers. Now, however, "I ask, have they not heard?" (10:18a)? They certainly have! "'Their voice has gone out to all the earth, and their words (the apostles' words) to the ends of the world.' But I ask (again), Did Israel not understand? First Moses says, 'I will make you jealous of those who are not a nation; with a foolish nation I will make you angry'" (10:18b–19). The obdurate Jews would burn in anger toward the Gentiles who gladly and eagerly receive the gospel. This is here prophesied. And through Isaiah, God speaks in prophesying words, which the Jews applied to the prophet as very bold and presumptuous, namely these words, "'I have been found by those who did not seek me; I have shown myself to those who did not ask for me'" (10:20); namely, the Gentiles. "But of Israel he says, 'All day long I have held out my hands to a disobedient and contrary people'" (10:21).

Let us return to the beginning of this letter and summarize. God, to be sure, does gather for Himself a people out of Israel that believes in the Savior and will be saved. But this people of God in Israel is, compared to the overwhelming mass of Israel, only a remnant, a small one at that. The great majority of Israel is obdurate, hardened, and has fallen prey to destruction. And how does one explain that? While blind heathen were converted and justified before God by faith, the highly advantaged Israel has rejected the gospel and thrown away from themselves the salvation which was so near to them and which was pressed upon them so urgently.

If anyone is converted and saved, then that is always and alone God's grace. But, if a person remains in unbelief, becomes hard of heart and is damned, then that is always and alone by his own fault. Learn this well here, Christian friends!

LETTER XXVI
GOD HAS NOT REJECTED HIS PEOPLE

Romans 11:1–10

We spoke of the Jews in the last four letters. We saw that this ancient and so highly advantaged people is banned from Christ and excluded from salvation because it remains in unbelief and hardens itself against the gospel. Now I ask, "Has God rejected his people?" (11:1). Surely it isn't that God does not want to have His people share in the salvation in Christ or come to faith in Christ, is it?

"By no means!" (11:1). Wasn't the apostle Paul himself a Jew "a descendant of Abraham, a member of the tribe of Benjamin" (11:1)? Yes. He was. So no, "God has not rejected his people whom he foreknew" (11:2). Those Israelites of the flesh which God Himself calls His people, should God have cast them away so mercilessly? That is even more unthinkable than that a mother should cast away her own baby. No, God did not cast away His people. He chose them for Himself already in eternity, elected them, and predetermined them for the salvation in Christ. Should God now have cast off these people? That's impossible!

But, dear Christians, think again of the heading of the Letter XXII (Chapter 9:1-13): "Not all who are descended from Israel belong to Israel" (9:6). Who are the people of God? Who are they whom He calls "His people"? Which people has God selected as His own from eternity? Is it the entire number of people, which after the flesh and outward ancestry are from Israel? Are these God's people? Does God call these His people? Did God select these for Himself already in eternity? Oh no! That people in national Israel, which according to the Spirit, according to the new birth from God, is the Israel of God, that—that alone is God's people! That true Israel, which was begotten out of the Spirit, that and that alone is God's people. These alone He calls His people, these alone God in eternity selected for Himself and designated for the salvation in Christ. "Not all who are descended from Israel belong to Israel" (9:6). You dare never forget this, my dear Christians! The true Israel which lies hidden in the national Israel, that is God's people. And these God did not cast away.

Or, "Do you not know what the Scripture says of Elijah, how he appeals to God against Israel? 'Lord, they have killed your prophets, they have demolished your altars, and I alone am left, and they seek my life.'" (11:2b–3). "But what is God's reply to him? 'I have kept for myself seven thousand men who have not bowed the knee to Baal'" (11:4). Do you see here the true Israel and people of God which lies hidden in the great mass of fallen-away Israel? Elijah didn't see it. But God did see it. God Himself permitted them to become that leftover remnant. God had rescued that remnant by His grace from the general, almost universal, falling away, unbelief, and perdition. There always has been a remnant in Israel, also today yet. So there always will be a remnant in Israel which God permits to be left over for Himself, according to His election of grace, in accordance with His selection in eternity. This is in conformity with His eternal and unfailing resolve and decree, according to which He appointed this remnant to faith in Christ and eternal salvation. And this remnant chosen by grace in Israel is that people of God, His people, which God has certainly not cast away.

Is anyone among you astonished at what has just been said? Does it sound strange or surprising to you? Does it seem offensive to some of you perhaps because I say that there is this remnant in Israel which God permits to become a leftover for Himself in accordance with His election of grace? A leftover remnant which God out of free grace alone has appointed to faith in Christ and eternal life, and that this leftover remnant is the people of God which God has not cast away? Perhaps some might suppose that I should have said that God already in eternity saw beforehand that there would be a remnant left over in Israel which would believe in

Christ. Or that this remnant which would conduct itself differently from the great mass of people, and have a different attitude from other people. And that God on account of this, by His foreseeing of their faith and better conduct and attitude, chose this remnant for salvation to be His people. Ah, but just a minute, friend. In the first place, remember I am speaking like St. Paul and all of Scripture. Secondly, when anyone is "leftover" or "a remnant" among the children of unbelief and of destruction, when someone comes to faith in Christ, is added to God's people, and is finally saved, then that is alone the doing of God's grace. It is alone the doing of the grace of God in time and eternity. It is altogether alone because of God's gracious operation in time and because of God's gracious will and predetermination in eternity. With God there is no happenstance, no sooner or later. With God everything is *now*. What God by His grace does in time, that He has predetermined to do by grace in eternity. Surely, you know that! So then, when someone by God's grace becomes a "remnant," a "leftover," then God has by His grace made him become a "remnant" or a "leftover." And God has in eternity by His grace determined and firmly decided to make just this certain someone a "remnant." He has chosen and ordained that this certain someone should become a remnant. In time as in eternity, it is by grace that a person becomes a remnant. "But if it is by grace, it is no longer on the basis of works." (11:6a), out of someone's "will or exertion," (9:16) out of someone's deportment. If that were the case, then "grace would no longer be grace" (11:6b); whole, full, pure grace. Surely, you can see that! But if it be of works—out of someone's "will or exertion," (9:16); if it be from something such as a better conduct, attitude, or being different which God had foreseen, which God had taken note of, "grace would no longer be grace" (11:6b). Surely, you would not want to deny that it is grace, would you? If so, then work would be no longer work, will and exertion would no longer be will and exertion, conduct and being different would no longer be conduct and being different. That means, then, the work—the will or exertion, the conduct and being different of the person—would no longer be the deciding factor, no longer be that by which God decided and determined to count people to be His people. It's either, or! Either you must let the conduct of people be the deciding factor and put away the "by grace" for time and eternity, or you must let the "by grace alone" be the one and only deciding factor and then put away the conduct of people. There is no third choice, no way, whatsoever! And now? How is it then in Israel's case? Like this, that for which the great mass of Israel is striving, they do not attain. After what is Israel striving? After righteousness before God and salvation. Why does Israel not attain it? Because it wants to attain it through its own works, not through the grace of God in Christ Jesus. "The elect obtained it" by grace (11:7).

And the rest? How about them? These were hardened and blinded by God as a just judgment upon them. In just judgment, God has finally hardened and blinded them because they, in spite of all the longsuffering work that God expended on them, would not believe. They hardened themselves against the gospel of Christ. That is the reason why God has now hardened them. "As it is written, 'God gave them a spirit of stupor, eyes that would not see and ears that would not hear, down to this very day.' And David says, 'Let their table become a snare and a trap, a stumbling block and a retribution for them; let their eyes be darkened so that they cannot see, and bend their backs forever'" (11:8–10), that they may have neither understanding nor strength to find salvation and walk the path of salvation.

So then, God did not cast away His people. But God's people are not the fleshly Israel or the Jews as a race or national people, but that remnant in Israel, which God permits to be leftover for Himself in all times according to the election of grace. And the others, in all times of world history, lay by their own overwhelming fault under the judgment of hardening.

And here let us find for ourselves a teaching for Christendom for that which is known as the Christian Church of today.

Letter XXVII
The Fall of the Great Mass of Israel Has Wholesome Consequences for Others

Romans 11:11–15

We have seen that God did certainly not cast away His people, that is, His true chosen Israel, but leads them with a strong, steady hand through faith to the promised eternal life. But the great majority, as we have seen of the people of Israel born according to the flesh, stumbled against Christ, the Rock of Offense, by their own fault and have fallen into destruction.

"So I ask, did they stumble in order that they might fall?" (11:11). Understand this question correctly. This is what is meant: the Jews who in their self-righteousness took offense against Christ and persistently hardened themselves against the gospel, these God in just judgment permits to fall into perdition. That is for certain. Yet, it surely is not that God now wants nothing more than that these fall into eternal perdition. It is certainly not so that someone could say, "The Jews harden themselves against Christ, the only Savior, and so fall into perdition. That's the whole of it, there is nothing further to it, nothing more of it." No, that's not the way it is. "By no means!" (11:11). God forbid that it is so!

But, how is it then? What is it that is meant to follow upon the hardening and fall of the great mass of Israel? Something wholesome, something salutary for others, something blessed indeed, for God's chosen and elect. For that is always the way our wonderful God works, that He makes healing and blessing come out of the evil and frightful things that His enemies do and bring upon themselves; blessing and salvation He makes to grow out of it all for His chosen ones.

What is that good blessedness? It is twofold. First of all, "Through their trespass salvation has come to the Gentiles"

(11:11). When the Jews set themselves against the gospel, the apostles turned to the Gentiles as the Lord commanded. And the gospel remained with the Gentiles. Multitudes of Gentiles received the gospel and so accepted the offered salvation. Secondly, because so many Gentiles believed and partook of salvation, Jews are again being enticed and urged to follow the example of the Gentiles and so also gain salvation. For not all Jews are finally and definitely hardened, even though they now for the present time lie in unbelief. God still has His elect ones also among the Jews. When these see the faith of the Gentiles and hear the gospel from them, the Holy Ghost makes "Israel jealous" (11:11), that they accept the gospel of Christ and believe. And so the number of elect in Israel will finally be full, the whole of God's people in Israel will be gathered in. Do you see it? This is how the good and salutary comes out of the unbelieving hardening of the great mass of Israel for others, by the grace of God, for the Gentiles and those elect hidden away in Israel.

But more still. If the fall of Israel, obduracy of the great mass of Israel is "the riches for the Gentiles" (11:12a), that the Gentiles thereby gain salvation; and if the loss, the destruction of Israel is the good fortune of the Gentiles, how much more will good and healing come by God's grace when the number of elect in Israel will be full? That is, when all the Jews shall have come to faith in Christ, whom God has from eternity selected. I shall presently show you what shall then come (11:11–12).

Note, I now speak to you Christians who in the great majority have descended from the Gentiles. Whoever has received a charge, a calling, to work among such in God's name, he should magnify and enhance his office and see to it that he perform his charge properly, so that the Gentile Christians be established in the faith and that even more of the Gentiles are converted. At the same time, one should have the design and purpose always to rescue and save some out of Israel. For this is the best way to do mission work among the Jews, that the Christians who live among the Jews, grow strong and firm in the faith and witness their faith by their deeds and behavior. Then, always some of Israel will be drawn to follow such a faith and will then also gain the salvation, as before said. And then, nearer and nearer will come that last good thing of which I wanted to tell you (11:14). "For if their rejection means"

(11:15) riches and salvation has come to the Gentiles, that many of them have received reconciliation with God by faith, wouldn't you think that something truly great and blessed beyond all measure would result, when finally all the elect of Israel shall have come to the faith and shall have been received into God's true people? And what would that be? Yes, what shall then come when the number of the elect of God's people in Israel shall be full? It is "life from the dead" (11:15). Then the whole great people of God which has been gathered together in all time out of Jews and Gentiles shall arise from the dead. The Lord's church shall greet and enclose into its blessed ranks the very last faithful ones of Gentiles and Jews who have lived to hear the last trumpet sound and the entire united throng of God's from-eternity chosen people. Not one lacking will then enter into eternal life and everlasting glory. Then one will hear a great voice from the throne of God and the Lamb, and it shall say, "'Behold, the dwelling place of God is with man. He will dwell with them, and they will be his people, and God himself will be with them as their God. He will wipe away every tear from their eyes, and death shall be no more, neither shall there be mourning, nor crying, nor pain anymore, for the former things have passed away.' And he who was seated on the throne said, 'Behold, I am making all things new.'" (Rev. 21:3–5a). That, my friends, is the "life from the dead" (11:15). That is the end and culmination of the blessedness, all the blessed consequences which by God's grace and governance have come and will come from the fall of the great mass of Israel.

Thus, our wonderful God operates always in His kingdom. If people in one place ignore, despise, and harden themselves against God's saving Word, and so cast themselves into perdition, then God permits healing and salvation to grow out of their fall for others. He then will send His Word to another place. He then lets it find acceptance there. He then gathers His children there and, yes, lets some in the former place where His Word was before despised be drawn that they will now also accept His Word and be saved. This is clearly seen in the history of the Christian Church. I don't want to present church history here, but I do want to draw your attention to America and Germany. God had given His Word to Germany like to none other land. Luther was a German. But, Germany despised God's Word. Germans then brought it to

America. It's here in America now. Then, some in the old fatherland were drawn to desire His Word again and will be saved, even as it is now going on in our day. Finally, then shall come the "life from the dead" (11:15).

Letter XXVIII
A Warning to Gentile Christians Lest They Boast Over and Against the Jews.

Romans 11:16–24

Since God has allowed the fall of the Jews to bring it about that the Gentiles gained salvation, we who are Gentile Christians might be tempted to boast of ourselves against the Jews. We might say, "Ah, forget about the Jews! We are the people whom God wants! God has cast off the Jews and accepted us." Perhaps, we might think like that. That, however, would be a very carnal way of thinking, totally wrong, and would not please God. Let us be warned of this!

Don't you know, Christian friends, that according to God's promise there are Jews right now who even though they today are held fast in unbelief, will finally by God's grace be brought to faith in Christ and be saved? Indeed there are such! But are you able to say who among others these are? No! But God knows them. They are God's elect, His chosen ones. And, therefore, before God they belong to the same dough prepared by God Himself of which the forefathers Abraham, Isaac, and Jacob are the very first, all this in spite of their present unbelief. "If the dough offered as firstfruits is holy, so is the whole lump" (11:16a). Or, let us say, "In God's sight, they are true branches of the olive tree planted by God Himself, Israel, of which the forefathers are the root." For, "if the root is holy, so are the branches" (11:16b). Do you, who now boast of yourself against the Jews, want to boast of yourself against these unknown ones who are, before God, true branches of the olive tree, Israel, even though for the time being they are still being held in unbelief (11:20)?

Think of the time of Christ and the apostles. There was a goodly number of Jews then, who in true faith, were waiting for the promised Messiah and were, therefore, true branches of the olive tree, Israel. But when Jesus stepped up before their eyes or was preached to them as the Messiah, they were offended at His lowly appearance, His cross, and did not believe that He was the Messiah. And so, because of their unbelief, they were broken off out of the branches of the olive tree. The Gentiles who were from a wild, unfruitful olive tree, were grafted in among the branches of the noble olive tree, became believers in Jesus, and so were made partakers of the root and sap of the olive tree, Israel. These Gentile Christians were now strongly tempted to boast themselves over against the Jews and these above-mentioned, broken-out branches.

What is the apostle Paul saying to such boastful Gentile believers? If I may explain in my own way, what he is saying is this: if some of the branches were broken out, but you who are of the wild olive tree, were grafted in among them, and have shared the root and sap in the olive tree, Israel, then "do not be arrogant toward the branches" (11:18). But if you still do boast, then you should know that you are not supporting the root, but the root supports you. Your faith, by virtue of which you possess salvation, did not come from you and from your fathers to the Jews. For you, together with your fathers and forefathers, are like a wild and unfruitful olive tree. But your faith is the faith which derived from the root and tree, Israel, and became yours. Of what then do you want to boast so proudly against the Jews and the broken out branches?

Someone might answer the apostle and say, "'Branches were broken off so that I might be grafted in'" (11:19).

The apostle answers, "That is true" (11:20). That's right. Through the fall of the Jews, salvation has come to you Gentiles. Since the Jews rejected the Gospel, it came to you Gentiles according to God's will and judgment. But consider this: the branches of whom you speak and against whom you boast so proudly were broken out because of their unbelief. But you stand on the olive tree of Israel through faith. And that faith is a faith presented to you as a gift, a poor-sinner faith, and cannot exist with pride and haughty conceit. So don't be proud and haughty, but be penitently afraid! "For if God did not spare the natural branches, neither will he spare you" (11:21). That is, He will not spare you if you deny the nature of true faith by your boasting. "Note then the kindness and the severity of God: severity toward those who have fallen, but God's kindness to you, provided you continue in his kindness. Otherwise you too will be cut off" (11:22). And those, the broken-out branches, if they do not remain in unbelief, will be grafted in again, for God is able to graft them in again, bringing them to faith in Christ (11:23). "For if you were cut from what is by nature a wild olive tree, and grafted, contrary to nature, into a cultivated olive tree, how much more will these, the natural branches, be grafted back into their own olive tree?" (11:24). Didn't they have the Word of God and the prophecies about Christ from the time they were children? Perhaps they were standing in the faith and were offended in Jesus only temporarily. So do not pride yourself in proud boasting over against the Jews, for there are God's elect among them. But fear because of your pride and abide in humble faith.

So spoke St. Paul. And let that be a warning also for us Christians today, lest we pridefully and boastingly brag of ourselves over against the Jews.

Three things we should here bear in mind. First, our eternal God considers all Jews as part of the true olive tree, Israel, who will finally yet come to faith in Christ Jesus, even though they at this time are still in unbelief. In like manner, God considers all men as members of His beloved church and assembly who at any time come to faith, even though they for time being are still without faith or perhaps not even born yet. Second, faith can be lost. And the lost faith can be recovered. A Christian can fall from faith and a fallen-away person can come to grace and faith again. Third, but how is this? Doesn't Scripture teach that we Christians and children of God should be absolutely certain of our security and permanence in faith and of our eternal election to salvation? How does the teaching that we can lose the faith and salvation agree with this? How does it agree also that God warns us of falling away? This cannot be explained with pen and ink or with theological formulas. Yet, true faith grasps it, nevertheless. The true and genuine faith says, "Lord, I am fully aware of my helplessness, also of the malice and wickedness of my heart. I humbly thank You for warning me. Yet, I am still Your dear child in spite of devil, world, and all sin. Save me through and in spite of it all! You have promised to rescue me. Save me! You have said that You have from eternity already chosen and determined to save Your own, to give them eternal salvation. You will save me too, in spite of all and give me eternal salvation. Amen! I doubt it not! No—I cannot doubt Your promise. Amen!"

Letter XXIX
"A Mystery Made Clear"

Romans 11:25–32

It actually appears as though almost all Jews were hopelessly hardened and blinded. We do not comprehend how God is going to accomplish this grafting in again of which we spoke in the previous letter. It is a mystery to us how God can have "a people" also among the Jews, which is being saved through faith in Jesus Christ, even as He has said and promised.

But it is this mystery exactly which the Apostle Paul does not want to hide, but wishes to reveal by inspiration of the Holy Spirit. This he intends to do lest we, by following our own blind smarts, might think that all Jews are hopelessly hardened, that God still would not graft any more Jews into the true olive tree of Israel, and that, therefore, the Word of promise that God spoke concerning Israel would not come true.

To clear up this mystery the apostle tells us three divinely established things. First, actual and hopeless blindness has overtaken unbelieving Israel only in part, but not all of them. Second, this is the condition (status quo) of unbelieving Israel until the full number of the Gentiles will have entered the Christian Church or until all the divinely elected Gentiles shall have been converted, in other words, until the Last Day. Third, just because many, but not all, unbelieving Jews are blinded beyond all hope, it still stands that "all Israel will be saved" (11:26) and will be converted and be eternally blessed. "All Israel," I say, which God calls His Israel from all eternity and to whom He gave the promise that out of Zion a Rescuer would come and turn away the godlessness from Jacob or Israel. And that this then shall be His (God's) covenant with him (Israel), that He shall take away and forgive Israel's sin. Of this Israel, not even one individual shall remain in unbelief, not even one shall be blinded beyond hope, not even one shall be lost. Every last one will be converted and be eternally saved. Such an Israel God has secured for Himself through all time until the Last Day. This is the Israel of the election, God's true Israel.

Dear Christian friend, is the mystery now cleared up and plain to you? Mark it well now, that not all Jews are hopelessly blinded. Mark it well how God again grafts in many unbelieving branches such as have been broken out of the olive tree of Israel. Do you now understand how God's Word of promise which He has spoken over His—I repeat, His—Israel, shall not fail but be fulfilled to the last tittle?

So then, how must we think of these unbelieving Jews? Looking at the gospel and at their hostile attitude toward it, we must certainly consider them enemies. Yet with it all, we certainly must gratefully remember how God made their enmity against the gospel serve for our blessing; namely, how He turned the gospel which they rejected to us Gentiles. But if one permits one's eyes to be enlightened by God's Word and focuses them upon the hidden people of God's election who are still concealed among the unbelieving Jews, who will still be converted and saved, then these are beloved ones, beloved of God and also our beloved ones. Such beloved ones of God are at all times among the Jews, "for the sake of their forefathers," (11:28), for the sake of the Word God gave to the fathers, Abraham, Isaac, and Jacob. That Word of God to the fathers is that God had chosen them as well as also their true seed and had called them, which means that He would also convert them. Such grace once given to the fathers, the grace (or gift) of election and calling, God shall never repent of. He will see it through to the end also with those Jews who at that time are still unbelievers. Ah yes, most assuredly! God will do so to the Last Day.

For just consider the Gentile Christians. Were not these also disobedient to God? Didn't they also willfully reject His gospel? And still they received mercy when God, because of the disobedience and unbelief of the Jews, turned the gospel to them, and they were converted. And is it not often so, that unbelieving mockers are by God's grace converted? Even so there are now, as always, Jews who are unbelievers, who yet will receive mercy and be converted. And this, to be sure, shall come about through the mercy that has been shown to us. Our faith, our confession, our Christian conduct, our witnessing—these God intends to use, that they be converted and be saved.

God first abandoned all His chosen ones in unbelief and has left them lying there in it as though hopelessly lost. But He has mercy upon all of them and brings them to faith, that His alone may be all the glory.

Don't ever rashly consider an unbeliever as hopelessly impenitent and lost, even though he rages and protests ever so madly and is ever so deeply fallen in sin. God may have entirely different thoughts concerning him. Continue witnessing to him, even with loving appeals and prayers.

In this manner, you must consider the people of Israel. They indeed seem to be a total anathema, a curse to God. And yet, as you have just seen, not all of them are hardened beyond all hope. God shall graft many a one in again. God's Word, which He has spoken concerning His Israel, has not failed, nor will it ever. God has a people of His choosing in the very midst of the obdurate Jewish people. They will obtain salvation!

Letter XXX
"Oh, the Depth of the Riches and Wisdom and Knowledge of God!"

Romans 11:33–36

"Oh, the depth of the riches and wisdom and the knowledge of God!" (11:33). So we must exclaim when we contemplate the things we have learned in Chapters 9–11 of Paul's Epistle to the Romans. Well, what was it we learned in these chapters? Let us see.

When God comes with His Word of grace, the gospel, He finds that the Jews as also the Gentiles are insubordinate to it, set themselves against it, and reject it outright. And yet God gathers for Himself a people out of such who become His very own by faith in Christ. And God does this so that He uses the unbelief of the Jews in such a manner that the Gospel which they reject is brought to the Gentiles. He uses the faith of the Gentiles converted by the gospel in such a manner that, in turn, the Jews emulate the converted Gentiles, turn away from their unbelief, and convert to the Christian faith. At the same time, however, God permits judgments of His wrath in the form of obduracy and destruction to come down upon such spiteful and self-hardening unbelievers. This He does, of course, only after He in "the riches and wisdom and the knowledge" (11:33) wills to do it. Nor can any man search out, learn, grasp, and say why God lets such judgments of wrath descend just at this or that time and just upon this or that individual before others. And with His chosen ones, God leads them on paths of grace only after He, in the riches of His wisdom and knowledge, wills to do it. No one can track down, understand, follow, and point out these paths of His grace in all their individual twists and turns. Nor can anyone say why God brought to faith in Christ and saved just this or that person before others, since all of them lie imprisoned equally in unbelief. In this manner, God rules this world. That is, He, in the unsearchable depths of His wisdom and knowledge, permits well-deserved judgments of wrath and guides in undeserved paths of grace until finally the whole council of His grace is carried out and brought into full reality for His elect and chosen ones. Then "life from the dead" (11:15) steps into full reality in God's kingdom of eternal glory.

This is what we have learned in these chapters.

And when one considers all this rightly and mediates upon it—I say, rightly consider and mediate up on it, not only read it over quickly and half understand or even misunderstand, then we must exclaim, "Oh, the depth of the riches and wisdom and knowledge of God! How unsearchable are his judgments and how inscrutable his ways!" (11:33).

Yes, even if we hold fast to it as divine and revealed truth, that God's judgments of wrath are always deserved by those upon whom they fall, and even if we also hold fast as equally divine and revealed truth that God's path of grace with His own can have their root and origin in God alone and never in ourselves and in our conduct and attitude, then the judgments of God's wrath as well as the paths of God's grace still remain incomprehensible and unsearchable to us. This was demonstrated before or much more as was laid out before us in our three chapters which we have now reproduced. God's judgments of wrath and also God's paths of grace rest and are grounded in the unsearchable depths of the riches of his wisdom and knowledge. They are and remain incomprehensible and unsearchable.

"For who has known the mind of the Lord?" (11:34a). Who has searched out the profundities of the Deity and there learned which opinion it was that guided the Lord in all His individual judgments of wrath and paths of grace? Certainly, no one!

Or who perhaps might have been His counselor or advisor so that he might have guided the Lord with this council in regard to the individual judgments of wrath or paths of grace and would now have a thorough understanding of them? A totally impossible thought!

"Or who has given a gift to him that he might be repaid?" (11:35). And should he, at least for his own person, know why God guided him on paths of grace and graciously spared him with His judgment of wrath? Listen up! Of each and every believer it must be said, "For all have sinned and fall short of the glory of God" (3:23). No, not one single Christian can say that his conduct and behavior in any possible manner was such that God was by it influenced to make just him one of His own.

But what other possibility of understanding the judgments of wrath and the paths of grace with the individuals does there remain after these three[10] are done away? None!

The judgments of God's wrath and the paths of God's grace are and remain unsearchable. They rest in the unfathomable depths of the wisdom and knowledge of God. Their origin, their first appearance, their goal and purpose are in God. "For from him and through him and to him are all things. To him be glory forever. Amen" (11:36). To Him be the glory given out of every believing, adoring Christian heart. To Him be the glory given which truly is due the Most High. Amen!

---

[10] The "these three" referenced here are referring to the three attempts—one in each of the preceding three paragraphs—to rationalize and understand why some people are eternally saved and others are not.

LETTER XXXI
"BY THE MERCIES OF GOD"

Romans 12

O, you Christians and children of God, how vast beyond measure is the mercy we have received and which we have come to know! God has made us lost and condemned sinners righteous by grace for Jesus' sake, without, yes, even in spite of our doing and merit, by faith alone, by which we cast ourselves alone on His Word of grace. And such a faith God has worked in us without any of our doing whatsoever. He has grafted us into Christ, so that Christ's life and power is operative in us unto a new life in holiness, in which we now progress toward eternal life in heaven. And in order to make it wholly clear and understandable that all this is only mercy and an eternal abyss of compassion toward us, God reveals to us that He already in eternity has elected and solemnly ordained us to all this, alone by grace, for Christ's sake. But not for the sake of anything else whatsoever, which might have somewhat distinguished us before others. Yes, how great is the mercy and compassion of God toward us and made known to us!

By this, His compassion, and His mercy toward us, are made known to us, and God now admonishes us that we give our bodies, our bodily life to Him. This is a sacrifice which is alive, active, busy, and holy coming out of believing and grateful, child-like hearts. Such a sacrifice is so well-pleasing to this God who loves us so. This should be our reasonable, our spiritual, our soul-desirous manner of worship. We should not imitate this miserable world in all our doing and dealing, planning and behavior, which neither knows nor cares to know anything of God's mercy. But we, who are still so much affected by sin and the doings of this world, should daily and constantly change and transform ourselves from the inside out, through the renewing of our minds. Then it should be that in all we do, we always first test and search out what in every case is according to God's will and in full agreement with what is good, God-pleasing, and perfect.

Dear children of God, does this admonition not fully agree with what is in your hearts? Most certainly, I'm sure!

And now, how should we, in conformity with this admonition, conduct ourselves in the Christian congregation with other Christians? Paul, through the grace of his apostolic office given to him by God, tells every one of us this. Here is what Paul has to tell us.

No one of us in a Christian congregation should think more highly than is exactly proper for him to think. Everyone should think very considerately and maintain the proper modesty and moderation in proportion to the measure of faith that God has given to each one. That is, the measure of cheerfulness, energy, and talent which flow out of faith in Christ to accomplish this or that in the congregation. For, in these gifts, there is considerable diversity among us Christians, "For as in one body we have many members, and the members do not all have the same function, so we, though many, are one body in Christ, and individually members one of another" in mutual relationship with each other (12:4–5). Here then we have varieties of gifts, according to the particular grace that has been given to us. If someone, for example, has "prophecy," the gift of divinely inspired oratory, then he should make use of it as corresponds to his faith, the measure of joyfulness, vigor, and ability of his faith. Of course, he should thereby remain very considerate and humble and be very much aware of what and how much has been given to him. He should not let himself become intoxicated by his gift, lest he think more highly of himself than he ought because of such a gift and undertake and attempt such things as are not given to him. So doing, he would render himself useless to both God and man. And, if someone in the congregation has been given the "service" (12:7), he should faithfully perform it in both teaching and admonishing. If someone has received the gift of giving, of sharing both temporal and spiritual things, then he should do it without show, motivated only by Christian love, not by desire for praise. If someone is directed to rule, in the church as elder or in the school as teacher or in the house as the father and mother, then let him do it carefully and zealously. If it has been given that someone "does acts of mercy" (12:8) to the poor, the sick, and needy in the congregation, let him do it with cheerfulness.

Especially within and without the congregation to which we belong, love should motivate and direct us in all our relationships, the love which we have received so generously from God. And this love should be genuine and sincere. This, of course, does not exclude but much rather includes and demands that we hate and reprimand the evil and cling to the good, seeking ever to lead the sinner to improve. Brotherly love among us Christians should be from the heart, this we must remember. We must also remember that the ties that bind us together in Christ are deeper and stronger than all ties of blood relationship. One should prefer the other more than himself and relate to him with due respect (12:10–11). In our dealing with our neighbor, we should not be careless and indifferent, but much rather be eager to serve him. Strive to be "fervent in spirit" (12:11), desiring to help and do good. But in all this, we should not proceed naively, but adjust to timely circumstances, providing help as needed and required. Even as we should for our own sakes be cheerful in our eternal hope and, therefore, be patient in tribulation and persistent in prayer, so we should also be concerned about the necessity of saints, so that their hope does not fail, but that their difficulty be overcome and their prayer be encouraged (12:12–13). So we should also gladly be willing to provide lodging, especially for the persecuted and displaced; yes, we should offer such hospitality eagerly. Should we ourselves be persecuted, we should bless our persecutors—bless, not curse (12:14). And as pertains to our brothers and fellow Christians, we should "rejoice with those who rejoice" and "weep with those who weep" (12:15). We should have the same mindset among ourselves and through love place ourselves into our neighbor's circumstances and empathize with him. We should not high-mindedly aspire to high and important positions, but in loving consideration hold ourselves to the level of the lowly. Do not deem yourself to be the only one who is wise nor take for granted that your opinion must always be the right one (12:16).

Regarding your conduct with the secular world, let love rule your behavior. We should repay no one evil with evil (12:17). We should concern ourselves with honesty towards everyone and conduct ourselves honorably in the eyes of all men. The eyes of the world are sharply focused on Christians. "If possible, so far as it depends on you, live peaceably with all" (12:18). Oh, dear Christians, "Never avenge yourselves, but leave it to the wrath of God" (12:19). He will avenge when and where it is necessary. Vengeance is His right alone, "for it is written, 'Vengeance is mine, I will repay, says the Lord.' To the contrary 'If your enemy is hungry, feed him; if he is thirsty, give him something to drink; for by so doing you will heap burning coals on his head'" (12:19–20). Your love will burn him and lead him to repent of the evil he has done to you. Don't be overcome by the evil done to you by your enemy, so that you, too, do the evil, but overcome evil with good (12:21).

This is the manner in which "the mercies of God" (12:1) admonish us Christians.

Letter XXXII
On Authority, Love of Neighbor, and Way of Life in the Light

Romans 13

Let every soul be subject to the supreme authorities under which he lives. A Christian should obey all governmental authorities and persons according to the legitimate laws and ordinances. It matters not of what form the government is, also not whether it has gotten its power justly or unjustly. When and however it came into existence, even so a Christian should submit himself to its rule. "For there is no authority except from God" (13:1). If God had not had to do with it, there would not be any government at all, nor could one be maintained because of the wild and unrestrained desire of the masses to run free. A Christian must, therefore, understand that the existing government is ordained by God. He, therefore, who pits himself against the government, he fights God's ordinance. And they that resist shall receive unto themselves the judgment, even the judgment of God (13:3). For you must also consider, rulers are not a terror to good, but to evil. The rulers and those having authority need not be feared because of good works, but of evil. But if you do not want to live in constant fear of the government, do good and you will have praise and favor. "For he is God's servant for your good. But if you do wrong, be afraid, for he does not bear the sword in vain. For he is the servant of God, an avenger who carries out God's wrath on the wrongdoer" (13:4).

Therefore, every Christian knows that it is necessary to be subject to the government, not alone for fear of punishment, but also "for the sake of the conscience" (13:5) toward God.

For this reason, also, you must also pay taxes, for the authorities are God's servants who are constantly occupied, as before said, in punishing the evil and protecting the good. "Pay to all what is owed to them: taxes to whom taxes are owed, revenue to whom revenue is owed, respect to whom respect is owed, honor to whom honor is owed" (13:7). Only in cases where the government clearly commands to do what God forbids, there applies the axiom, "We must obey God rather than men" (Acts 5:29).

Yes, we Christians should give to all what we owe them. We should owe no one anything. There is only one debt which we can never consider paid in full, namely, our love to the neighbor. This debt will be one we owe through our whole life to our very last word we speak to our neighbor, to the last glance we can give him. The Word of God requires ever and always that we love our neighbor. He who loves his neighbor has fulfilled the Law, "For the commandments, 'You shall not commit adultery, You shall not murder, You shall not steal, You shall not covet,' and any other commandment, are summed up in this word: 'You shall love your neighbor as yourself'" (13:9).

Love will do the neighbor no evil, but only and ever good. "Therefore love is the fulfilling of the law" (13:10b). Love is the one thing God requires of us, as pertains to our conduct to our neighbor. All the individual commandments are nothing more or less than expressions of love. Ever and always, I repeat, God requires of us that we love our neighbor. And we Christians are being admonished to it "by the mercies of God," (12:1) as we have seen in the previous letter.

And, dear Christians, seeing that time, "that the hour has come for you to wake from sleep" (13:11), that we whom God at one time has awakened out of the sin-sleep of death, constantly arise from the sleep of sin which would overpower us weak people so easily. Yes, indeed, this we must remember to do. For our salvation, our eternal salvation, is now nearer than when we first became believers and by faith came to know God's grace in Christ. "The night," the night of this earthly life, our life in the flesh, "is far gone; and the day," however, the day which shall bring us the eternal glory and perfection, "is at hand" (13:12). "So then let us cast off the works of darkness" (13:12); God, of course, will give us the strength to do so "and put on the armor of light" (13:12). Let us not do things that belong to the darkness of unbelief. Let us go forward to the eternal day in putting on armor and weapons that befit the light of God, the light of faith which enlightens us. Let us fight valiantly in this armor which God provides us daily, against the devil, world, and flesh, who want to pull us back into the night and would make us unworthy of the eternal day. "Let us walk properly as in the daytime, not in orgies and drunkenness, not in sexual immorality and sensuality, not in quarreling and jealousy" (13:13). Much rather, let us "put on the Lord Jesus Christ" (13:14), putting on His manner of life, His walk in the light and become ever more and more like Him in virtuous living, following Him in all things.

> I am the Light, I light the way,
> A godly life displaying;
> I bid you walk as in the day,
> I keep your feet from straying.
> I am the Way, and well I show
> How you must sojourn here below.
>
> I teach you how to shun and flee
> What harms your soul's salvation,
> Your heart from ev'ry guile to free,
> From sin and its temptation.
> I am the Refuge of the soul
> And lead you to your heav'nly goal.[11]

So, we Christians must put on Christ and follow Christ. And the concerns for our bodies, which of course are just and right, we should not seek in such a way that the evil desires of the flesh are thereby aroused.

To this we are admonished "by the mercies of God" (12:1).

---

[11] Angelus Silesius (Johann Scheffler), "'Come Follow Me,' the Savior Spake," stanzas 2 and 4.

Letter XXXIII
How the Strong in Faith and the Weak in Faith Should Conduct Themselves with Each Other

Romans 14

In Christian congregations there may well be those of strong faith and those of weak faith. By strong in faith are meant those Christians who out of God's Word are completely confident that for Jesus' sake they are standing in God's grace. Their life also is certain in God's Word, meaning, they let themselves be governed and led alone and wholly by God's Word in their life and conduct, and are certain that they are doing what is right and pleasing to God. These are the Christians that are as they should be. By the weak in faith, such Christians are meant who also find comfort in the grace of God in Christ offered them in God's Word, but with somewhat trembling hearts. And as concerns their life and conduct, they indeed also follow the Word of God, but in order to do that, they think that they must also still have all sorts of human props and crutches, which are not exactly suggested to them by God's Word. The gracious God loves these Christians even as a proper mother loves her weak child. This difference between the strong and the weak in faith will be made clearer in the following discussion.

First off, it's taken for granted that God desires it that the weak in faith should be fully and completely received in the Christian brotherly fellowship. One should not pitilessly criticize their thinking and scruples and qualms which they have, by which only a lot of confusion of conscience and disunity would arise in a congregation.

Here, for example, is one who believes and has the confidence well grounded in God's Word that he may eat anything and everything he pleases. Another one, however, who is weak in faith, eats only vegetation, because he is afraid that eating meat makes the body too voluptuous, arouses evil desires and, therefore, is not pleasing to God. Now what? He who eats everything should not despise him who does not eat everything. And he who does not eat everything, should not judge him who does eat everything, for God has accepted this one as His servant and dear child. Judge him? "Who are you to pass judgment on the servant of another" (14:4)? He stands or falls, as pertains to his manner of life, before Him Who is his Master. He will stand even though he does not follow your thinking and ideas, for God can well see to it that he stands.

Or, "one person esteems one day as better than another" (14:5) for private prayer, devotions, and study of God's Word, and for other spiritual exercises, because he believes that such practices are necessary for a Christian. Another person selects, I might say, every day, and so provides for his soul's welfare, but regards no day different from the rest. How about this? Well, each should be persuaded in his own thinking. Each should be convinced in his own mind that as he is doing it, it is for himself wholesome and good. He who prefers one day to the other, he does it so to his Lord. He who does not prefer one day to the other, he also does it to his Lord. So it is also with the aforementioned eating. He who eats everything, he does it so to the Lord, for he thanks God by so doing. He who does not eat everything, he also does it so to the Lord, and is thanking God by doing like that. For none of us who are Christians, "lives to himself," and none of us "dies to himself" (14:7). "For if we live, we live to the Lord, and if we die, we die to the Lord. So then, whether we live or whether we die, we are the Lord's. For to this end Christ died and lived again, that he might be Lord of the dead and of the living" (14:8–9).

But you, "why do you pass judgment on your brother" (14:10)? Because he does not consider these peculiar things as you do? Or, how about you, why do you despise your brother because he regards such peculiar things as important for himself, which you do not? Christ the Lord is the One, He Who knows all of us and before Whose judgment seat all of us will have to stand (14:10). "For it is written, 'As I live, says the Lord, every knee shall bow to me, and every tongue shall confess to God.' So then each of us will give an account of himself to God" (14:11–12).

"Therefore let us not pass judgment on one another any longer" or despise one another anymore. Rather, judge this and keep a sharp eye out for this: that no man "put a stumbling block or hindrance in the way of a brother" (14:13).

Look, fellow Christians, we can know and be sure in the Lord Jesus that no food in itself is common or polluting, that is, harmful for the Christian life. But, when someone considers it common, harmful for the Christian life, for him it then is common, that is, harmful. If someone considers eating flesh to be sinful, he then also sins if he eats flesh, for then, you see, he is doing something which he judges to be sin. And when your brother, because of your flesh-eating, is first grieved but then misled in that he also eats flesh, that is, that he then does something which he considers sinful; when he by your example is made worse—then, you are obviously not dealing with him out of or motivated by love. Out of love, I say, which is in the kingdom of Christ the fundamental law for life in every respect. Do not by your uncharitable eating of flesh or by anything else, destroy him for whom Christ gave His life.

And then let us also keep in mind in this matter, the unbelievers outside of the congregation! Should they notice that we Christians are quarreling among ourselves over eating and drinking, they will be given an opening to make fun of our precious faith and to mock it (14:16). Therefore, let us take care that this our precious gem is not so sullied! For certainly, the kingdom of God is not a matter of eating and drinking, but of righteousness before God through our Lord Jesus Christ, and of peace with God and of joy in the Holy Ghost. These are the true and genuine treasures of the kingdom of God. He who has these and then serves Christ in sincerity, he is pleasing to God and of beneficial value to people. Such Christianity is of a kind that it also draws attention among unbelievers and, God granting His grace, it causes them to do some thinking (have some second thoughts) which could lead to great spiritual blessings for them. Therefore, let us not quarrel over outward things, over things neither commanded nor forbidden in God's Word. Rather, strive for those things which bring and serve peace and improvement, mutual edification (14:19). But we really do not want to speak of the unbelieving. That just came in by chance. Let's get back on track.

Your bother was redeemed and converted by God through Christ! "Do not, for the sake of food, destroy the work of God" (14:20a). But that is really what you would do if you, by inconsiderate and loveless use of your Christian liberty, would offend and cause him to fall, as stated before. "Everything is indeed clean, but it is wrong for anyone to make another stumble by what he eats" (14:20b). This occurs when his conscience tells him it is sinful to do so. Surely, you are also aware of that now. So then, it is well and good if you do not eat meat, and drink no wine, or do anything else, at which your brother is offended or stumbles or because of which he may become weak and so does something against his conscience and conviction (14:21). You truly believe and are convinced by God's Word, that you may eat and drink anything and everything. Right you are! But, have this confidence in yourself before God! Do not use this, your faith and confidence, to injure your brother with it. That one is truly blessed who does not have a bad conscience in doing, eating or drinking what he permits himself to do, eat, drink, or whatever. But he who doubts whether it is right, and eats, nevertheless, he is condemned if he eats, because he does it not out of faith. "For whatever does not proceed from faith is sin" (14:23). What one does not do out of confidence that it is right before God, whatever one does with a doubting, trembling wounded conscience, that—regardless of how it may seem in and of itself—is sin (14:23).

In this letter, dear Christians, nothing is mentioned of the false-teaching Jewish Christians. These people wanted to impose upon Christians as necessary for salvation the keeping of the entire Jewish ceremonial Law. Nothing is said also of people such as the Temperance people and the Blue Laws people, who want to make a sin out of the enjoyment of beer and wine and teach that Sunday must be observed as the Jews observed the Sabbath in the Old Testament. Such people must be opposed loud and clear. Yet, St. Paul is not speaking of such here. Here we are speaking of dear Christians and children of God who would gladly serve God and now believe they have to avoid this or that and must set aside such and such times for special devotional exercises. To such one should give room and not grieve them or even cause them to lose their faith by inconsiderate use of one's Christian liberty. And we should here learn that the use of indifferent things, things which

God neither commands nor forbids, are sin when one does them with an offended conscience or when one does them and thereby offends the conscience of a weak Christian. Understand this clearly! But, I repeat what I explained before: when high-minded, holier-than-thou people wish to command or forbid us some indifferent thing as though God said so, then we should defend our Christian liberty and oppose them loud and clear.

Letter XXXIV
Christians Should Bear the Frailty of Weakness and Love God in Unity with One Another

Romans 15:1–13

All those who bear the name "Christian" rightly, who really and truly believe on the Lord Jesus Christ, all those are God's dear children whom God enfolds with His fervent love. That must be firmly noted.

Among these God-beloved people, as shown in the last letter, there are such who are strong in knowledge of the faith and such who are weak in the same.

Among these God-beloved people there are, however, also such who are strong and robust in the Christian life and conduct, who even though sin still clings to them, nevertheless withstand sin with quiet and confident certainty and walk in God's ways. Such have received great grace indeed and are to be envied! And there are likewise among them such who, as pertains to the Christian life and conduct, still have many weaknesses and imperfections. These are still feeble in their life and conduct, and are much like people who have just recently recovered from a typically fatal illness, not yet able to stand and walk right, much less able to accomplish very much. But God loves them just the same and bears them on in their frailty with tender patience, and wants to better them and strengthen them.

Now, since God is so concerned about these weak Christians, what sort of an attitude ought those strong Christians have toward these? Well, isn't the answer already given in the question? Isn't everyone already aware of it?

"We who are strong have an obligation to bear with the failings of the weak" (15:1). Strong Christians ought to live as though these infirmities were their own, and seek to improve and strengthen the weak with great love and patience. They should not live only to please themselves, or only concern themselves with making sure their own walk and conduct is pleasing to God. He who lives only to please himself is not right with God.

"Let each of us please his neighbor for his good" so he will be edified (15:2). Look on the Lord Jesus Christ! He didn't live to please Himself, but concerned Himself so much with the sinners and the feeble and the impotent that the godless and hypocrites reviled and reproached Him, saying, "This man receives sinners and eats with them" (Luke 15:2) and "Look at him! A glutton and a drunkard, a friend of tax collectors and sinners!" (Luke 7:34). Christ Himself had foretold that this would happen to Him in Psalm 69:9b where He said, "the reproaches of those who reproach you have fallen on me." You see, this was spoken of Him long before it actually happened. But "whatever was written in former days was written for our instruction" (15:4a). By this longsuffering, patient, putting up with the many weaknesses of our weak brother—which often is so tiresome and so contrary to our own flesh and blood—Holy Scripture works in us patience, strength, and the hope of eternal life, and also for our weak brothers. For Holy Scripture is a powerful spiritual force and a writing through which Christ is transfigured in our hearts, a power by which Christ is clearly portrayed in our hearts as He verily is, in fact. Yes, that very God, Who works such patience and comfort through His Holy Scriptures, may He bring it about that we, the strong and the weak may be like-minded toward one another after the manner of Jesus Christ and according to His will; namely, that the strong bear with the frailties of the weak and the weak let themselves be carried and helped and improved (15:5). All this "that together you may with one voice glorify the God and Father of our Lord Jesus Christ" (15:6), Who, with our beloved patient Redeemer is of such one and the same friendly disposition toward us. Such glorifying of God is surely the very breath of faith, and the right worship of God, with which God is well pleased.

Therefore, in order that such glorification of God may rule and increase more and more among us, we should receive one another in love, the strong the weak, the weak the strong, "as Christ has welcomed you, for the glory of God" (15:7). So the Holy Spirit admonishes us through the Apostle Paul.

In this manner, the Holy Spirit once admonished the Jewish Christians and the Gentile Christians in Rome. The Jewish Christians He admonished, who from childhood up knew the Holy Scriptures and so should have been strong, and the Gentile Christians, who from childhood up had served idols as they were led, and of whom one would, of course, sooner have expected that they would be weak. The Holy Spirit clearly showed both of them how Christ received both of them. He showed them how Christ first served the Circumcision, the Jews, namely, how He first off called the Jews to His salvation through His own preaching and then through the preaching of the apostles. And this He did for the truth of God to confirm the promises made to the fathers, the Jews, that the salvation should be brought to their offspring. Consequently, the converted Jews now glorify God for His divine mercy (15:9). But Christ also served the Gentiles; the Gentiles He also called to His salvation by the preaching of the gospel, and so also the converted Gentiles should glorify the divine mercy. And even this, too, had been prophesied in the Scriptures of the Old Testament. For the Messiah spoke in Psalm 18:49, "For this I will praise you, O LORD, among the nations, and sing to your name." And again God said, " Rejoice, O Gentiles with his people" (15:10), with the converted Jews. And again in Psalm 117:1, "Praise the LORD, all nations! Extol him, all peoples!" And again Isaiah says, "The root of Jesse will come, even he who arises to rule the Gentiles; in him will the Gentiles hope" (15:12).

Even so Christ has also today received us who are Christians, both old and new ones, firmly established ones and fearsomely wavering ones, strong and weak. And so we should receive one another among ourselves in order that one and the same praise of God should sound forth out of all our hearts.

That God, however, who gives to us the hope of the eternal glory, may He fill all of us "with all joy and peace in believing" in our Savior, Jesus Christ, who has completely reconciled us to Him (15:13). All this that we might be fully and richly blessed in the hope of the eternal glory "by the power of the Holy Spirit" (15:13).

Letter XXXV
An Afterword

Romans 15:14–33

Dear Christians! I wrote letters to you out of the Epistle to the Romans and have assiduously endeavored to speak to you with the greatest possible clarity and plainness—and at time my manner of speech has been rather bold and sharp—but I did not do so in order to pretend to be your teacher. For I know all too well and see ever more clearly with glad surprise that so many of our servants in the Word and also so many of our hearers are outstanding, "filled with all knowledge" and are very able indeed to teach and "instruct one another" better than I can (15:14). All that I wanted to do was to remind you in the form of commonly understood language of that which the great apostle Paul writes to the Romans, much like any preacher presents the divine Word to his congregation, explains it and applies it to them for their use. And so I thought it would be a good thing to expound to you in these letters the teachings or doctrines of this great Chief of Epistles, the Epistle to the Romans, to speak Paul's words after him. You should not consider these letters anything but just that.

And the Apostle Paul himself, what does he say in these concluding remarks in his epistle to the Romans? He calls his readers "brothers" and says, "I myself am satisfied about you, my brothers, that you yourselves are full of goodness, filled with all knowledge and able to instruct one another" (15:14). But he has, nevertheless, written to them, and with some rather bold words at that, as one who wanted to remind them of the divine truths and verities. And all this, "because of the grace given me by God to be a minister of Christ Jesus to the Gentiles" (15:15b–16a), to, "in priestly service," discharge his duties with the gospel, in order that the Gentiles might become a living sacrifice, acceptable to God, "sanctified by the Holy Spirit" (15:16).

Paul also says that he has "reason to be proud of my work for God" (16:17). The glory is in Christ Jesus, in things pertaining to divine service as an apostle, not, however, in matters of his own person and work. He did not want to be presumptuous, speaking boastfully of something, except of that which Christ accomplished through him, namely to bring the Gentiles to the obedience of faith by word and deed through the power of signs and miracles performed by the all-present virtue of the Holy Spirit (15:18). And so he had fully preached the gospel of Christ in wide areas into Illyricum (15:19). And he was intent on not preaching the gospel to places where the name of Christ was already known, for he did not want to "build on someone else's foundation" (15:20). He wanted to do as it was written, "Those who have never been told of him will see, and those who have never heard will understand" (15:21).

The fact that Paul wrote his letter to this congregation in Rome which was founded by others does not disagree with what he said above. As an apostle, he had the total authority, as already indicated, to do that. Nor was it against his principles to say that he had oft-times desired to visit this congregation. But, he says that the heavy work load he had among those who had not yet heard the gospel was the reason why he was prevented from doing as he would have liked to do. But now that he has no more place in the areas which he has already visited; that is, since they are now filled with preaching and that of other apostles, he would like nothing better than to come to them on his way through to Spain. On his trip through to Spain, he hoped to see them and then to be led by them to Spain, after enjoying their good fellowship. But first now he must go to Jerusalem to minister to the saints there (15:25). "For Macedonia and Achaia have been pleased to make some contribution for the poor among the saints at Jerusalem" (15:26). They were delighted to do this and indeed, they were indebted to them. For, if the Jewish Christians shared their spiritual treasures with the Gentiles, the Gentiles have a clear duty to contribute to their material needs. So when he would have finished this task and have delivered to the Christians in Jerusalem this gift of brotherly love, then Paul would travel to Spain via Rome (15:27–28).

And he was certain that when he does visit them he would come to them with the fullness of Christ's blessing (15:29), and that Christ would bless them richly through his, that is, the apostle's word.

Paul did go to Jerusalem, not with fear, but with considerable apprehension. He wondered whether the gospel-hating Jews would waylay him; yes, even that the gift of love he was delivering might not be pleasing to all the Christians there (15:30–31). This latter concern explains itself in this: Paul knew that in the congregation in Jerusalem there were those who were caught in the Jewish delusion that Gentiles had to become Jews before they could become Christians, and also had to keep the Jewish ceremonial Law after they had so become Christians. And since it was common knowledge that Paul did not hold to this teaching, but even opposed it vehemently, it was to be feared that many in the Jerusalem congregation would oppose him, the gift-bearer, as well as also the gift itself which he was bringing, because it had come from Gentile Christians. So he pleaded with the Roman Christians that they would help him do battle in prayer for him to God, that he would be delivered from the unbelievers in Judea, and his service designated for Jerusalem would be acceptable there to the believers (15:30–31). He wanted so much to be able to come to Rome with joy, if it be God's will, to be refreshed there and recuperated in their Christian fellowship (15:32). And for this intercession he begged of his Christians in Rome "by our Lord Jesus Christ and by the love of the Spirit" (15:30), because through the Lord Jesus Christ all Christians are bound together much more closely than by bonds of blood relationship or of friendship. And the love which the Holy Spirit generates among Christians is the most sincere and most firm of all. There is none like it.

Well, Paul really did come to his dear Christians in Rome, but in quite different circumstances than he would have humanly expected: as a prisoner, a persecuted one, to be sure, and despised, but a rescued prisoner, nevertheless. God leads His own in most miraculous ways, but he leads them with a strong hand to the promised goal.

Paul closes the afterword of his letter to the Romans with the words, "May the God of peace be with you all. Amen" (15:33). And, God, reconciled to us through Christ, wants to give to all Christians both temporal and eternal peace, great peace without end. Dear Christians, permit me to greet you also with this divine greeting.

LETTER XXXVI
POSTSCRIPT

Romans 16

Even as we often add one or more postscripts to our letters, so Paul also did when he wrote his Epistle to the Romans.

First, he commended to them Phoebe, who very likely was the bearer of this epistle. Phoebe was a deaconess in the congregation in Cenchrea, a suburb and port city of Corinth, where St. Paul wrote the epistle. He calls her "our sister" and asks the Christians in Rome that they receive her in the Lord, as it befits the saints, and that they would stand by her in any business in which she may need their assistance, because she had stood by many others, including St. Paul (16:1–2). Christians should open hearts and doors to each other and lend a helping hand whenever necessary.

Then, St. Paul sends greetings to certain Christians with whom he was personally acquainted, or to such of whom he had heard by name. Firstly, to Priscilla and Aquila, the Christian couple, known to every Bible reader, especially from the Book of Acts (16:3). Paul notes that they risked their necks to save his life. Not only he, but all the congregations among the Gentiles would like to thank them for this (16:4). They now resided in Rome, and gathered in their house a portion of the congregation for regular divine worship (16:5). At that time, it was not yet possible to have public church buildings, instead there were so-called house-churches in members' homes. Also, these he greets in his letter. Then he sends greetings also to many unknown to us, but who we shall know someday in heaven: a certain Gentile Christian, Epaenetus, the first convert to Christ in a Roman province (16:5), a certain Mary, who spent much time and labor on Paul and his company (16:6),

Andronicus and Junius[12], fellow countrymen of Paul, and comrades with him in captivity for Christ (16:7). These he refers to as "well known to the apostles" and of whom he says that they were Christians before he was (16:7), a certain Ampliatus, whom he loved "in the Lord" (16:8), Urbanus, a fellow worker in the work of Christ, a beloved Stachys (16:9), a tried and true Apelles, the household of Aristobulus (16:10), his relative Herodion, those converted to Christ of a certain Narcissus (16:11), a Tryphaena and Tryphosa who work in the Lord's service, a dear Persis who had worked hard in the Lord (16:12), a certain Rufus, perhaps the son of that Simon, who carried the cross for Christ, and whose mother, whom he also calls his mother (16:13), Asyncritus, Phlegon, Hermes, Patrobas, Hermas and the Christians gathering with them (16:14), a Philologus, and a Julia, a Nereus and his sister, and Olympas and all the Christians gathering with them (16:15).

And then Paul adds that they should greet one another with the holy kiss (16:16). It was the oriental custom for a man to greet the man, and the woman the woman, by kissing the cheek. This kiss was to be to the Christians a sign or symbol of sacred fellowship, of Christian love in the Lord Jesus Christ. Then follows a goodwill greeting from all, to all congregations.

Oh, that such heartfelt brotherly love were also freely burning among us present day Christians!

The Roman congregation was still free of teachers of false prophets. But are we not aware of the fact that right here in Rome the falsest of all false prophets would arise, the Roman antichrist? And, did not St. Paul in spirit see, how even now already the "mystery of iniquity" was showing itself, how he at least was already planning to gradually change the old Roman world domain into that Roman pope-domain, holding all Christendom in its thrall? That is the reason why his heart breaks, as it were, for the congregation in Rome, warning them above all, of what would come, saying, "I appeal to you, brothers, to watch out for those who cause divisions and create obstacles contrary to the doctrine that you have been taught; avoid them. For such persons do not

---

[12] At the time that Zorn published this commentary, there were not yet any questions about this name. Though this volume follows the ESV, the name Junius is preserved as Zorn would have known it.

serve our Lord Christ, but their own appetites, and by smooth talk and flattery they deceive the hearts of the naïve. For your obedience is known to all, so that I rejoice over you, but I want you to be wise as to what is good and innocent as to what is evil" (16:17-19).

"The God of peace will soon crush Satan under your feet" (16:20).

The one and only safeguard against the corruptions of the Roman antichrist and all other doctrinal corruption is a pure, single-minded sincerity, with alert foresight in respect to the teachings of Christ.

And now, Paul delivers greetings from individuals who were with him, especially Timothy, his faithful helper, and Lucius, Jason and Sosipater, his relative (16:21).

The heart of Tertius also, to whom Paul dictated this epistle, moves him to add in his own words, "I, Tertius, who wrote this letter, greet you in the Lord" (16:22).

Then Paul continues to dictate, "Gaius, who is host to me and to the whole church greets you." Paul lived with Gaius in Corinth, and his house was always open for all Christians. "Erastus, the city treasurer, and our brother Quartus, greet you." (16:23).

And, as if he could not express his love adequately, he again adds, "The grace of our Lord Jesus Christ be with you all. Amen" (16:24).[13]

The epistle is now finished, right? No, not yet! A word of praise to God through Jesus Christ must still be added, "Now to him who is able to strengthen you according to my gospel and the preaching of Jesus Christ, according to the revelation of the mystery that was kept secret for long ages but has now been disclosed and through the prophetic writings has been made known to all nations, according to the command of the eternal God, to bring about the obedience of faith—to the only wise God" (16:25-27a)—Paul was going to say "be honor through Jesus Christ," but when he came to Jesus Christ, he interrupted his paean of praise and gave to Jesus Christ, to the only begotten Son of the Father Who is with the Father, one Being and one Divine Majesty, the

---

[13] Romans 6:24 is only included as a footnote in the ESV.

honor and glory and said, "be glory forevermore through Jesus Christ! Amen" (16:27).

Ah yes, glory to God through Jesus Christ! He has brought about salvation for us, He strengthens and upholds us in the healing and saving faith through His Word and Holy Spirit, He alone. To Him be the glory! Amen.

Made in the USA
Middletown, DE
09 February 2020